MILITARY TO CI

EMPLOYMENT

A Career Practitioner's Guide

Yvonne Rodney

Military to Civilian Employment: A Career Practitioner's Guide

Copyright © 2016 by CERIC
All rights reserved. No part of this publication may be reproduced or
transmitted in any form or by any means, electronic or mechanical,
including photocopying, recording, or any information storage and
retrieval system, without permission in writing from the publisher,
Canadian Education and Research Institute for Counselling (CERIC).

Published and distributed in 2016 by
Canadian Education and Research Institute for Counselling (CERIC)

Canadian Education and Research Institute for Counselling (CERIC)
2 St. Clair Avenue East, Suite 300
Toronto, Ontario, Canada M4T 2T5
Tel: (416) 929-2510
www.ceric.ca

Library and Archives Canada Cataloguing in Publication

Rodney, Yvonne
Military to civilian employment – a career practitioner's guide / Yvonne
Rodney.

Also available in ePUB format.
ISBN 978-1-988066-08-0
Book Design: Communicreations.ca

A military career teaches leadership, discipline, dedication, teamwork and offers its members a vast array of highly transferable skills. These men and women add immediate value to any civilian organization. As the leader in Military transition, Canada Company is proud to stand shoulder to shoulder with those that do the heavy lifting for us every day.

—Blake Goldring, Canada Company[1]

Table of Contents

From the Publisher

For the last few years, we have been hearing that career professionals across Canada are seeing more clients from a military background. These Canadian Armed Forces personnel exit the military each year and face unique challenges and opportunities in successfully transitioning to civilian careers and further educational opportunities. Career professionals have indicated that they are in need of a specialized resource they can use in helping veterans make the transition to meaningful and satisfying work in the civilian labour market. As a national charitable organization that supports the development of resources that enhance the work of Canadian career professionals, the Canadian Education and Research Institute for Counselling (CERIC) recognized the importance of meeting this need. We therefore set out to create a suitable resource in English and French. *Military to Civilian Employment: A Career Practitioner's Guide* is the result.

In developing this resource, CERIC found a welcoming partner in Canada Company and its Military Employment Transition (MET) Program. Canada Company is a charitable organization founded, funded and supported by the Canadian business community to serve our military exclusively with a direct line on the specific needs of Canadian businesses, and how military resources can be the secret weapon. Indeed, this project would not have been possible without the critical support and encouragement provided by Canada Company. They helped to enlighten and clarify, and to connect many of the dots, as it were. They were also critical in helping us secure Knowledge Champions whose financial support ensured that the project could be realized.

In addition to Canada Company, our special thanks to the following Knowledge Champions for their leadership in supporting the project: British Columbia Institute of Technology (BCIT); Canadian Career Information Association (CCIA); Fanshawe College; G. Raymond Chang School of Continuing Education, Ryerson University; Marine Institute of Memorial University; Northern Alberta Institute of Technology (NAIT); TriOS College; and Wilfrid Laurier University. Their support ensured the development and dissemination of the guide.

The guide's author, Yvonne Rodney, had the mammoth task of gathering content, synthesizing information and framing materials within an evidence-based career development lens. She consulted and collaborated with the Canadian Armed Forces, Veterans Affairs Canada, Military Family Services, military-friendly employers, CAF veterans, and front-line career professionals. Each of these actors played a critical role in ensuring that the final product was a resonant one.

Lastly, the support of the CERIC Board of Directors was essential to ensuring that the germ of an idea could flourish into a much-needed and widely accessible resource. A special thank you to Robert Shea who championed this project at the CERIC Board.

The challenges and opportunities in successfully transitioning from military to civilian employment require a well-versed career professional. This guide will equip career professionals with what they need to know to assist former military personnel in moving to prosperous careers after serving their country. This is important not only for individual veterans and their families, but for the entire Canadian economy.

— Riz Ibrahim, Executive Director, CERIC

Acknowledgements

This guide would not have been possible without the assistance and expertise of the following champions:

Dwayne L. Cormier, Canada Company, steadfast champion for the creation of this guide. Thanks for providing access to resources and transitioning personnel, and for your overall tireless efforts to assist in the military-to-civilian transition. The transitioning military members valued your personalized approach and asked for "more like you" to be available. Out of that request came this guide, to equip other career practitioners to do what you do.

Jo-Anne Flawn-LaForge, Canadian Armed Forces (CAF) Transition Advisor, Career Transition Services, for providing context, content and feedback about life in the military and CAF Career Transition Services.

Suzie Bouchard, B.S.W., M.Ed., CD1, Joint CAF–VAC Initiative at Veterans Affairs Canada, for providing content and feedback.

Katie Ochin, Military Family Services, CAF whose rich knowledge of CAF families framed the information about the career needs of military spouses.

Melissa Martin, B.A., B.Ed., a military spouse and bilingual, certified counsellor, who provided input on military-relevant strategies, approaches and tools.

Lisa Taylor, Challenge Factory, who when she heard about this resource offered to share information about how the Legacy Careers® Approach could benefit transitioning military personnel.

CAF veterans and spouses, for providing feedback and case stories. You continue to embody the core principles of military life: reliability, responsibility, respect, efficiency and service orientation. Thanks for adding flavour to the guide.

Marilyn Van Norman, National Coordinator, Outreach and Innovation, CERIC, for coordinating process and project alike. You kept us all moving in the most respectful ways.

Career practitioners, service providers, educators and researchers who advocate, document, raise awareness and provide support for those who ensure our borders are secure and our peace is defended.

From the Author

What kind of life comprises military service? Why do people join? Why do they stay? Why do they leave? And when they leave, what do they need to successfully transition to civilian employment?

This guide is meant for career practitioners who know little about life in the military. I write it intentionally in a collegial tone, as if we were sitting together in a comfortable room sharing good information.

From a content perspective, I am not attempting to tell you how to do the great job you already do or to tell you all there is to know about life in the Canadian Armed Forces. Rather, see this book as a reference and use it to better understand the unique employment-related needs of former and current military members who might seek your professional assistance.

The guide also provides an overview of how families support the military member, the challenges in providing that support, and best practices for career coaches and counsellors working with military spouses/partners.

Military to Civilian Employment is informed by a comprehensive review of the identified career needs of veterans, interviews with former and current Canadian Armed Forces servicemen and servicewomen, and an assessment of service gaps.

My favourite part of the research was the conversations with current and former service members. Their politeness, their reliability, their responsiveness, and their willingness to contribute really impressed me.

I hope you find the information useful.

—Yvonne Rodney

Reader's Guide

In the busyness of our work there isn't always time to read a book from cover to cover. With that in mind, I have written this guide in such a way that you can start at any chapter that catches your attention. As a result you may notice that some bits of information are repeated in more than one chapter. That way you don't have to always go back to a previous chapter to get the information you need. Here are a few quick notes to help you make the most of the reading:

Who Is the Guide About?

This book is primarily about transitioning members or veterans of the Canadian **Regular Forces** and members of the **Reserve Forces**, with a chapter on military families. Regular Force veterans would have been employed full-time within the Canadian Armed Forces (CAF). Reservists are part-time soldiers who provide support to the Regular Forces domestically or internationally. They typically serve part-time (evenings/weekends) and hold down full-time civilian jobs. They may also apply to serve on full-time contracts similar to those of members of the Regular Forces.

A **veteran**, as defined by Veterans Affairs Canada, is "any former member of the Canadian Armed Forces who successfully underwent basic training and is honourably discharged."[2]

Features of the Guide

Terms: The terms veteran, soldier, military member and serviceman/woman are sometimes used interchangeably. Note the context. Both male and female veterans are referred to throughout, and pronouns alternate.

Chapter Contents: You will be told the content of each chapter right up front.

Key Learning: Important points are listed at the end of each chapter.

Stories: The experiences of real CAF servicewomen and servicemen are interspersed throughout the guide. Names and other personal identifiers have been changed.

Yvonne's Favourites: Resources or news items that I find particularly useful are listed at the end of each chapter. Not all chapters have this feature.

Initialisms and Acronyms: See Appendix 2 for a list of military initialisms and acronyms used in the book. The following appear frequently:

CAF – Canadian Armed Forces

DND – Department of National Defence

VAC – Veterans Affairs Canada

Useful Statistics and Information

Canada's Defence Team is made up of the following numbers (2013)[3]:

- Regular Forces – 68,000 members
- Reserves – 27,000 members
- Civilians – 24,000 members

The Canadian Armed Forces comprise three main environments:[4]

- **SEA** – Royal Canadian Navy:
  8,400 full-time;
  5,100 part-time sailors
- **LAND** – Royal Canadian Army:
  21,000 full-time members;
  20,000 Reservists;
  5,000 Rangers (a component of the Reserves)[5]
- **AIR** – Royal Canadian Air Force:
  13,365 full-time airmen and airwomen;
  2,035 Reserve airmen and airwomen

The "purple trades" provides support to all three environments of the CAF in the areas of logistics, resource management, human resources and technicians. Members in the purple trades can work within all three environments regardless of uniform designation.

A Woman Walks Into Your Office

A career in the Canadian Armed Forces is a call to duty. The soldiers, sailors, airmen and airwomen who through the years have answered this call exemplify many of the values that define and unite Canadians from coast to coast. They possess the desire to help others and a will to fight for and protect what they believe in.

The Canadian Armed Forces is a unique organization where members learn and develop combat and combat support skills. There are no lateral employment transfers from outside. Career progression is based on experience and knowledge acquired through training and employment within the Canadian Armed Forces itself. It is a career like no other.

Of the 95,000 Regular and Reserve members, approximately 5,000 leave the Canadian Armed Forces each year. Many of these members, especially those spending a number of years in service, have little or no experience of the civilian job market.[6]

In July 2014 the Canadian Senate's Subcommittee on Veterans Affairs released a comprehensive report, *The Transition to Civilian Life of Veterans*, which included a series of recommendations to address the needs of personnel transitioning from the Canadian Regular and Reserve Forces.[7]

That same month, the US-based Career Planning and Adult Development Network dedicated the entirety of the Fall 2014 issue of its *Career Planning and Adult Development Journal* to addressing the needs of US veterans. What these reports, along with my interviews of current and former CAF members, revealed is that in addition to the challenges of returning to civilian life, the transition to civilian careers and employment has its own set of reintegration challenges.

Canada Company, through its Military Employment Transition (MET) Program, is an example of a non-military organization dedicated to helping CAF veterans transition to civilian employment. (A listing of such organizations can be found in Chapter 8 inclusive of a few new and promising initiatives.) That said, with approximately 5,000 personnel leaving the CAF annually, sooner or later one of them will end up in your office or mine.

This is the reason for this career practitioner's guide. It is meant to provide context, background, useful tools and resources to help us in our work with this population.

Enough preambles. Let's get started!

❊ ❊ ❊

Consider this fictitious scenario:

A woman in her late 30s walks into your office. She tells you that she's been a soldier for the last 18 years and has recently left the Canadian Armed Forces. She's looking for work and needs your advice.

You know how to do this. For years you've been helping clients find meaningful employment or helping them assess, determine or clarify their career aspirations. You know how to create measurable goals, target resumés, empower clients in articulating and demonstrating their competencies, or even advise on how and where to get additional training if needed. You can show them how to do effective networking using all the social media and direct contact resources available. The task before you is easy. First you find out who they are, what they've done, and what kind of work they aspire towards. You might also review their resumé to better understand their work history prior to helping them formulate a work-search strategy.

But when you read this client's resumé it becomes clear that she is a little bit different. She's been an artillery soldier. Terms like howitzers, M-Triple-Seven, forward observer, prepping the ammo, and pulling the lanyard leave you completely befuddled.

So you ask: "How did you get into this line of work?"

Answer: "Well, after high school I didn't know what I wanted to do with my life. Someone suggested going into service so a friend and I went down to the CAF recruiting office and registered. I successfully completed my basic training and decided to become an artillery soldier."

You ask a follow-up question: "What exactly did you do?"

Answer: "Well, I did a number of job-related tasks to support combat missions, specifically indirect fire support, air defence, and surveillance and target acquisition in battle."

Huh?

You try again: "Can you speak specifically to the type of work you enjoy and personally excel at?"

Answer: "I really enjoyed the more advanced weapons-handling, field-craft, and section-level tactics."

This is not going well at all.

Another question: "So tell me, what made you decide to leave your military career?"

Answer: "Well, after multiple postings across the country, it was getting increasingly difficult for my children to adapt to new schools, new friends, etc."

❋ ❋ ❋

While the above is a fictitious scenario, it highlights some of the challenges faced by transitioning military personnel in articulating what they bring to the workplace.

There is much about military life that is not known to those who have not lived it. So before we embark on helping our client find civilian employment, let's learn a bit about the areas of need and the life she's leaving behind.

PART I:
NEEDS AND CULTURE

Photo credit: Canadian Armed Forces

Former Forces members bring with them management skills, ingenuity, discipline and a common sense of purpose that the private sector needs.

—Blake Goldring, Canada Company[8]

Understanding the Needs

The decision to leave military service, whether voluntary or involuntary, will entail some adjustments. In a 2014 report prepared by the Senate's Subcommittee on Veterans Affairs, 25 percent of veterans interviewed between 1998 and 2007 reported experiencing difficulty in transitioning to civilian life.[9]

Members who have left the CAF may experience a loss of identity. They may miss the authority they exercised or the discipline of the military environment. For many, the Canadian Armed Forces provided a goal-oriented, driven and structured lifestyle. Members wore a uniform that denoted their standing and their commitment to their country. They experienced challenges and adventures found in few other work environments. These are some of the rewards of service in the CAF. When a member leaves the military, they leave all of this behind.

One former service member interviewed bemoaned the fact that no one talks about these losses. For her, giving up her badge was the hardest part of leaving. It meant giving up her membership in the military community and all the accompanying rewards.

Because life in the Armed Forces provides so much support and identity to its members, career practitioner Melissa Martin suggests, where possible, an 18-month timeline for transition planning before release. CAF Transition Advisor Jo-Anne Flawn-LaForge goes even further: She encourages Regular Force members to start their transition planning five years out from release.[10]

Why such a long time?

The longer a member was in the Forces, the longer the adjustment period might be. Veterans have to come to terms with life in the civilian world and, if necessary, take time to grieve the things they miss about military life. The veteran has to readjust to family life, look for work as opposed to being appointed to a position, possibly retrain for a different job or go back to school, adjust to a civilian work culture—to name a few. That's why preplanning is so critical.

One of the veterans I interviewed in 2014 for a CERIC report concurred: When asked "What was your biggest challenge (in adjusting to civilian careers)?", the veteran's response was, "Needed to get on with the prep earlier. Never started prep till it was upon me. Six months to a year would be recommended."[11]

It's just like retirement planning: the greater the advance planning for life after service, the easier the transition.

Okay. We now know there are losses. We know there are adjustment challenges. What about the needs of veterans? A review of the literature in Canada and the United States reveals nine general categories of need.

An Overview of Needs and Challenges

1. Understanding Military Culture

That most civilians, inclusive of career practitioners, educators and employers, do not understand the nature of military life, culture and training means that myths and ignorance are perpetuated. In the 2014 special Veterans issue of a career development journal, Krysta Kurzynski reports that US veterans feel that civilians have a lack of understanding and appreciation of the work they have performed for their country.[12] I'd hazard a guess that CAF veterans feel this way too.

Canada Company, Canadian Armed Forces Career Transition Services, Veterans Affairs Canada and others understand the value former service members can bring to the workplace and so concentrate a portion of their work on educating employers about military culture and how it already equips its members with competencies needed in civilian workplaces. That said, the average Canadian probably knows more about the US military than they do about our own Canadian Armed Forces. That's another reason for this guide. We tend to disregard or prejudge that which we do not understand. From the terminologies, ranks, and structure to the different types of work environments and what each does, greater public understanding of military life will help ex-service members more easily transition to the civilian job market.

How about educational institutions offering military-friendly courses and inviting vets to contribute their real experience to the curriculum and classroom?[13] This could be a way to show support and appreciation for what soldiers have to deal with as well as broaden knowledge. Regardless of one's position on the ethics of warfare, bridging the gap between the military and civilian worlds will eliminate at least one of the many obstacles these public servants face on returning to civilian life.

2. Supports/Networks and Outreach

Veterans benefit most when they have a support network—connections to people who speak their language, understand what they've been through, and can provide training, mentorship, employment, links to employers, and information about available support services. An interesting recommendation suggests training veterans to be Global Career Development Facilitators (GCDF) so they can help their peers.[14] Not a bad idea.

The greater the extent to which family members, career practitioners, professional associations, service providers as well as veterans collaborate in sharing knowledge, resources and best practices, the fewer former servicemen and servicewomen will be neglected.

3. Services for Ill or Injured Veterans

Imagine the plight of the soldier who has not chosen to leave the CAF but must. He has been injured; he knows the drill. A member of the CAF must be ready to perform a broad range of tasks, not just the duties of his specific occupation, and the fact that he can no longer meet this Universality of Service principle means he can no longer wear the uniform.[15] Leaving is hard enough—especially if that identity meant a lot to him. Now, on top of all the aforementioned losses, this veteran has to deal with the losses associated with the injury itself. How does this affect work and life on a daily basis?

The most consistent finding in all CAF mental health research is that most members are free of mental illness during any given year. A significant minority will, however, have problems during a given year, and a much larger group will suffer from a mental illness at some point in their lives. The 2002 CAF Mental Health Survey showed that 15 percent of all CAF personnel had experienced symptoms of one of five common mental disorders in the previous 12 months: major depression, social phobia, post-traumatic stress disorder (PTSD), panic disorder, and generalized anxiety disorder.[16]

Studies have demonstrated that the overall prevalence of one or more mental illnesses in the CAF is similar to that in the general population. The same is true for the level of alcohol dependence. For reasons that are not yet fully understood, however, CAF Regular Force personnel have almost twice the risk of depression than do their civilian counterparts.

While most medically releasing members do not have a workplace-limiting injury, recent warfare has seen an increase in the number of reports of operational stress injuries (OSIs) inclusive of post-traumatic stress disorders (PTSDs) and traumatic brain injuries (TBIs).[17] Other manifestations of mental illness affecting military members include depression, anxiety disorders and substance abuse.

What of limiting physical injuries? Career practitioners can be that much more helpful to ill or injured veterans if we have at least a rudimentary knowledge of these disabilities and the resources available to support those who have them.

4. Education and Training

If one entered the CAF with only a Grade 10 education and worked in a very military-specific type of job, it is more than likely that some degree of further education or retraining will be needed on leaving military service. Many, however, do not know what relevant benefits are available, how to access or use them, or even where to study. This is why it is critical for members to connect with CAF Career Transition Services prior to leaving.

Then there is the credentialism issue. How do service members with military credentials and training leverage them in civilian life? Do institutions give credit for military training, courses or work experience? If yes, which ones? What documentation is required? How do we easily disseminate this information to veterans? We will look at some answers to these questions in Chapter 6.

5. Employment

Richard N. Bolles, author of the popular job search guide *What Color Is Your Parachute?*, asserts that finding employment is the single most important need of returning veterans.[18] In a 2015 New York Times article, it was reported that prior to leaving the military, 70 percent of US veterans felt confident they would be successful in obtaining jobs once they left service.[19] However, one year after they were out, the number feeling confident had dropped to 57 percent and then to 46 percent the following year. In the areas of creating resumés, writing effective cover letters, networking, and translation of skills, they reported feeling ill equipped and ill prepared to compete with non-veterans for jobs. Furthermore, coming from a culture where promotions are based on performance or seniority, even the standard job interview is unfamiliar territory.

While the labour market outcomes for CAF veterans are, on average, fairly positive, there are subgroups experiencing challenges similar to those faced by US veterans.

Chapters 3 and 4 will cover the topic of employment in more detail, but here are some of the key employment-related needs identified in the literature:

- Job finding information inclusive of a step-by-step plan

- Job search tools and resources specific to veterans

- Addressing employer myths/fears about hiring veterans or those returning from a tour of duty who might be called up again

- Translating military jobs into civilian workplace language

- Information on civilian/military job equivalencies
- Overcoming obstacles to employment (under-education, financial, disabilities)
- Constructing civilian resumés; accessing professional coaching and writing services; preparing for civilian job interviews
- Dealing with work-culture transition e.g., moving from hierarchy and conformity to self-promotion
- Accessing jobs and military-friendly employers
- Income drop upon transition

6. Skill Translation

Another area of need that goes hand in hand with employment is how to apply skills used in the military to civilian careers. A related challenge is identifying civilian job equivalents for military occupations. Furthermore, it would be useful if more career practitioners were knowledgeable about the trends in career areas for which veterans would have had previous training. More on that later.

7. Unique Career Development Issues

The nature of military service, and the potential impact of warfare on those who fight, may result in this population of workers having needs that are different from the norm. We already touched on the needs of those with physical and mental health issues that are directly attributable to their service in the military. We noted how important it is for veterans to connect with those who understand military life and culture. There is also a need for career professionals with expertise in working with the military population. For those who are novices in this area, this guide is but one step. We can also engage military members in helping us understand military life.

8. Services and Supports for Military Family Members

The deployment (assignment away from home) and relocation of military members affects their families too. With every move, the partner of a military member needs to find a new home, set it up, register children in a new school, apply for the transfer of medical records, make new friends, and find a new job. In Chapter 7 we will examine the impact of the military lifestyle on a spouse's career development and employability.

9. Research and Assessment

The Life After Service Studies (LASS) seek to understand the effects of the transition from military to civilian life on CAF veterans. The 2013 LASS provides important information on the post-release employment of CAF veterans.[20] However, there is much yet that we do not know. Longitudinal data comparing different military populations and how each transitions is needed. More research on the needs of female veterans, the unique challenges of reservists, understanding transition, how to enhance coping and adaptation, as well as tools and methodologies career practitioners can use is important.

Finally, how are current interventions working? What tools are available to measure the effectiveness of services? What benchmarks are being employed? When all is said and done, are our CAF veterans being well served? That is the ultimate goal.

So there you have it—a look at the needs and challenges! Those most directly related to helping CAF veterans in their journey from military to civilian employment will be the focus of the rest of this guide. Now let's turn our attention to the topic of military life and culture.

* Career practitioners should address
  the losses experienced by veterans
  when they leave military service.

* Finding work is the single biggest challenge
  faced by veterans as they return to civilian life.

* Veterans have unique career development
  needs that career professionals
  must seek to understand.

* Other needs/challenges for those transitioning
  to civilian life, as identified in the literature: a
  lack of understanding of military culture outside
  the military, a need for supports and networks,
  access to supports and services for ill and injured
  veterans, access to and information about
  education and training, the ability to translate
  skills to civilian careers and determine civilian
  job equivalents, services and supports for family
  members, more research and assessment.

Yvonne's Favourites
*Life after Service Studies (LASS). The
2013 report, which includes statistics on
the post-release employment of veterans,
is chock full of great information.*

As a group, [veterans] are generally more disciplined, punctual, mission-oriented, and team-oriented than the population at large.

—Richard N. Bolles[21]

"It's a different world"

Raymond served in the Canadian Armed Forces for over 26 years, and by the time he left he was a Major in the Armour Corps.

His reason for joining? "My father was in the Army and I wanted the same type of challenges and exciting life."

He left because he got injured.

"I miss the people, the way we plan and the way we interact with each other," says Raymond.

Now that he is on the civilian side of life he works in the area of business development.

"I started with one firm, but after eight months realized the fit was not right and have moved to another company."

His former army colleagues, Canada Company and completing his MBA helped him transition. "The biggest adjustments are the people, the way they interact with each other and the planning or lack of planning that I have encountered so far in the business world."

Raymond's advice to those about to leave military service for a career in the civilian world is to network and to always be ready to help people in a positive manner. "You never know when it will pay off or how you helping someone today will help in the future. Building a large network where you connect people and bring solutions to big and small problems inside and outside of work is key to transitioning.

"It is a different world and the social dynamic and office politics are an adjustment. There is work out there, wait for a good fit and be prepared to move to find it. Job, title, pay, benefits, home life, holidays, and more are all elements that in my mind move like an equalizer up and down; they cannot be all up in reality and you must make sacrifices or at least choices to have different combinations.

"Big money will take hard work and probably lots of time away from family. If vacation and being home every night is more important, then you will likely not make as much money. Finding the fit that matches your needs and personality and the needs of your family are key to your happiness.

"Getting it right the first time right out the gate from the Army is difficult and not realistic. Spend the time before you leave to figure out what you want to make it as likely a fit as possible."

CHAPTER 2

Understanding Military Culture

Joining: The Path to Becoming a CAF Member

To join the Regular Forces, one must be:

- A Canadian Citizen
- 17 years of age (with parental consent) or older. Older applicants must be at an age to complete training and at least one term of service prior to the mandatory retirement age of 60.
- A graduate of Grade 10 (Quebec Secondaire IV) or higher
- Eligible to hold a security clearance

To join the Reserve Forces, one must contact a local reserve office for a list of available positions and then apply online.[22] Applications are processed locally.

Educational requirements

While Grade 10 is the minimum requirement, most jobs within the Regular Forces require completion of high school or its equivalent.[23] If one has completed college, university and/ or has a number of years of work experience, they could potentially qualify for a reduction in the length of their military training through a Prior Learning Assessment.

Medical assessment

All applicants are assessed by a team of medical professionals to determine any restrictions that would affect their ability to serve.

Basic training

After being accepted by the CAF, all personnel must undergo basic training at the Canadian Forces Leadership and Recruit School in Quebec. This training teaches the skills and knowledge required to succeed in the military. It includes physical fitness, basic military skills, handling a weapon, first aid, and military values/ethics. Those on the Officer track must take the 14-week Basic Military Officer Qualification course and those who are non-commissioned members take the 12-week Basic Military Qualification course.

Length of service

Length of service is typically for a term of three years but might be longer based on the need for one's skills and the duration of training required. If the CAF pays for a member's training, the length of service will be longer.

Serving: Military Life and Culture

The Canadian Armed Forces (CAF) and the Department of National Defence (DND) form the Defence Team of Canada, employing over 100,000 military and civilian employees. This is the largest federal government department and its purpose is twofold:

1. Protect Canada and Canadians from any challenges to its domestic security.

2. Help to uphold Canadian values internationally as directed by the elected government.

The CAF is responsible for defending Canada, contributing to the defence of North America, and contributing to international security. DND acts as the support system for Canadian Armed Forces operations—base services as well as operational and corporate support.

DND/CAF Senior Governance

- **The Governor General,** not the Prime Minister, is the Commander-in-Chief of Canada and is responsible for appointing the Chief of Defence Staff at the recommendation of the Prime Minister and for awarding honours and badges, the presentation of Colours, approving military badges and insignias, and signing commission documents.

- The **Minister of National Defence** acts as CEO for the Department of National Defence and manages all matters relating to national defence. This person is a federal Cabinet Minister.

- The **Associate Minister of National Defence** is responsible for defence files as instructed by the Prime Minister and ensures that CAF members have the equipment and materials needed to do their jobs. This person is also a federal Cabinet Minister.

- The **Deputy Minister of National Defence** is responsible for policy, resources, interdepartmental coordination and international defence relations.

- The **Chief of Defence Staff** is the senior serving Officer of the CAF. He or she is responsible for the overall command, control and administration of the Forces in addition to military requirements, strategies and plans.

Rank Structure

Ranks denote responsibility, status and accountability. It is essential to the discipline structure of military life. The culture of the CAF is unapologetically hierarchical. The chain of command is the necessary spine that supports operational effectiveness and discipline. A Code of Values and Ethics outlines the principles, values and expected behaviours of CAF members.[24] Acceptance of and adherence to the Code of Values and Ethics is a condition of employment within the CAF.

The overall job of the commanding officer is to make decisions, provide directives and support to subordinates, respect the chain of command and be accountable for the actions of subordinates. It is the job of subordinates to implement the orders issued by their commanding officer.

Within the CAF, there are 19 ranks and two types of soldiers: commissioned officers (COs) and non-commissioned members (NCMs).

Commissioned Officers:

Officers must be capable of commanding; developing policies, plans and programs; training units to accomplish designated tasks; and providing the right conditions and environments for the NCMs to do their jobs effectively. To become an officer one needs the required level of university education or enrolment in the Regular Officer Training Program.

The head of the Officer rank in the Canadian Armed Forces is the Admiral/General who serves as the Chief of Defence Staff and is appointed by the Prime Minister from the group of military members having the rank of Vice Admiral/ Lieutenant-General.

As you can see from the table on **page 42**, the Army and the Air Force both use the same naming convention to identify ranks. The Navy is different. Some ranks in the Navy do not correspond to ones in the Army or Air Force. For example, a Navy Captain is three levels higher in rank than a Captain in the Air Force or Army. This puts the Navy Captain on the same level as a Colonel in the Army or Air Force. Navy emblems have an added "N" beside the titles of Captain or Lieutenant. The chart on **page 44** provides a pictorial depiction of ranks and insignias.

CAF Rank Structure

Chief of Defence Staff		
NAVY (Black uniform)	**ARMY (Green uniform)**	**AIR FORCE (Blue uniform)**
COMMISSIONED MEMBERS		
General Officers		
Admiral	General	General
Vice-Admiral	Lieutenant-General	Lieutenant-General
Rear-Admiral	Major-General	Major-General
Commodore	Brigadier-General	Brigadier-General
Senior Officers		
Captain	Colonel	Colonel
Commander	Lieutenant-Colonel	Lieutenant-Colonel
Lieutenant-Commander	Major	Major
Junior Officers		
Lieutenant	Captain	Captain
Sub-Lieutenant	Lieutenant	Lieutenant
Acting Sub-Lieutenant	Second Lieutenant	Second Lieutenant
Subordinate Officers		
Naval Cadet	Officer Cadet	Officer Cadet

NON-COMMISSIONED MEMBERS		
Senior Appointments		
CAF Chief Warrant Officer	CAF Chief Warrant Officer	CAF Chief Warrant Officer
Chief Petty Officer	Command Chief Warrant Officer	Command Chief Warrant Officer
Formation Chief Petty Officer	Formation Chief Warrant Officer	Formation Chief Warrant Officer
Senior Ranks		
Chief Petty Officer 1st Class	Chief Warrant Officer	Chief Warrant Officer
Chief Petty Officer 2nd Class	Master Warrant Officer	Master Warrant Officer
Petty Officer 1st Class	Warrant Officer	Warrant Officer
Petty Officer 2nd Class	Sergeant	Sergeant
Junior Ranks		
Master Seaman	Master Corporal	Master Corporal
Leading Seaman	Corporal	Corporal
Able Seaman	Private	Aviator
Ordinary Seaman	Private (Basic)	Aviator (Basic)

CAF Insignia

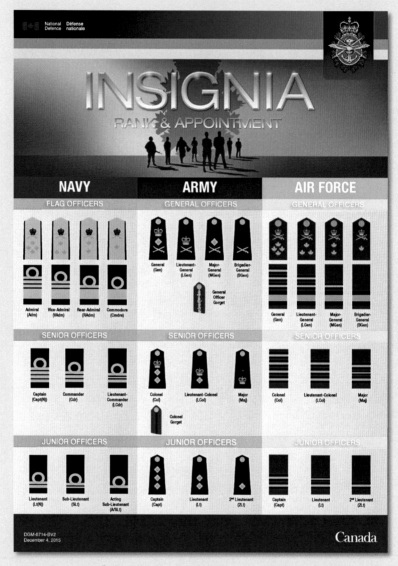

Property of the Canadian Armed Forces. Used with permission.

CAF Insignia

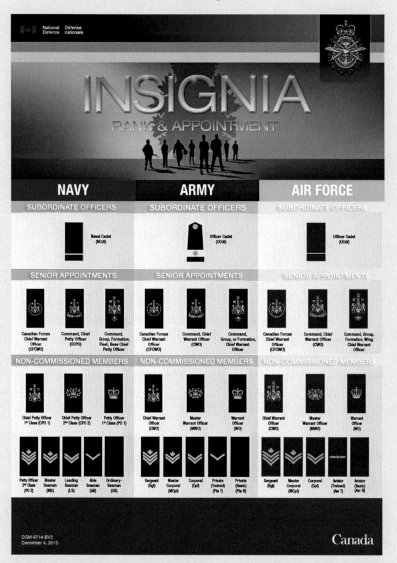

Non-commissioned Members:

These members are lower in rank than Commissioned Officers and do not hold a commission. This segment of the CAF is divided into eight ranks, with Chief Petty Officer (Navy) and Chief Warrant Officer (Army and Air Force) being the highest-ranked NCMs.

Non-commissioned members can apply to become Officers under different commissioning programs. If accepted, they are required to complete a university degree if they don't already have one. In addition, those who have attained the rank of Sergeant or one of the ranks in the Warrant Officer group and who have demonstrated strong leadership skills could be offered a commissioning from the ranks, which, if accepted, places them in the Junior Officer group of the Officer structure. This group is not required to obtain a university degree.

Note: Many NCMs have no desire to become Officers. Chief Warrant or Chief Petty Officers are at the top of their field with extensive influence and span of control to affect change. Many Majors (Senior Officers), depending on their occupation, do not have that same level of responsibility. Leaving this sphere of influence to go into a Junior Officer group where they are at the bottom of the Officer structure is not appealing to many.

Occupations

While ranks denote standing within the CAF hierarchy, each serving member has his or her own distinct job. There are over 100 occupations in the military falling into 10 broad categories. Each category comprises Officers and non-commissioned members and requires specific education and/or training. There are more than 30 Officer careers in the CAF and 70 NCM occupations.[25] Fields of speciality include:

- Administration and Support
- Combat Specialities
- Engineering
- Health Care
- Sensor and Radar
- Public Protection
- Telecommunications
- Technicians
- Air and Ship's Crew
- Other (Chaplain, Musician, Cadet Instructor, Intelligence Operator, Intelligence Officer, Legal Officer and Imagery Technician)

Mindset

From the first day of basic training, it has been drilled into each member that priority is always given first to one's mission, then to one's fellow members, and last to one's self. In other words, service before self. Duty, loyalty, integrity and courage are foundational tenets of this culture. A soldier must also be prepared to work irregular or extended hours if needed, and to perform under extreme physical stress. In line with the "soldier first" mentality, mobility, deployability, and physical fitness are key expectations of military work life and culture. (More on this below.)

Mobility/Postings

A serving member of the CAF can expect to be posted several times during their career. Postings indicate promotions or advancement through the ranks. Promotions are typically done at the discretion of the commanding officer and are based on seniority and performance. Postings usually take place during the spring and summer but may vary based on organizational needs.

Deployment

With fairly short notice, a CAF member can be called upon to undertake a specific mission. This means that the member must always be in a state of readiness: to work, if the nature of the mission requires it, irregular or long shifts; to use any mode of transportation; to eat infrequently or miss meals; and to perform under extreme physical or environmental stress and even with little or no medical support. Both body and mind must therefore be in top shape at all times. Deployability and employability go hand in hand: When a member is no longer able to meet the Universality of Service or "soldier first" principle, he can no longer wear the uniform.[26]

Physical Fitness

Fitness is another key requirement of military life. Time is allotted to each CAF member each day to work out. Members must take and pass a physical fitness test each year or more frequently, depending on the specific requirements of their work.

Competencies and Skills

Each serving member must be able to fire and maintain a personal weapon, conduct drills, fight fires, perform first aid/CPR, communicate using radio technology, prepare written correspondence and demonstrate the following core competencies:

- Personal motivation
- Planning/initiative
- Teamwork
- Client service
- Order and quality
- Critical thinking
- Subject matter expertise
- Flexibility
- Influence
- Continual learning
- Organizational awareness
- Self-confidence
- Self-management
- Leadership
- Responsiveness

Education, Training and Professional Development

Educational opportunities and continuous learning are accessible once one joins the CAF. Each military member has the opportunity to establish personal learning plans whereby they can hone skills or develop new ones. However, the CAF member who is employed full-time needs to balance taking courses alongside that full-time work commitment.

There are three institutions of learning associated with the Canadian Armed Forces:

- **The Royal Military College of Canada (RMCC)**
  [www.rmcc-cmrc.ca]. Located in Kingston, Ontario, RMCC prepares Officer cadets and naval cadets for careers in military service. It also accepts civilian graduate and undergraduate students who are interested in learning about defence issues. Its primary role is that of educating and developing leaders who want to serve Canada through the CAF.

- **The Royal Military College Saint-Jean**
  [www.cmrsj-rmcsj.forces.gc.ca]. Located in Saint-Jean-sur-Richelieu, Quebec, this college prepares students who have potential but are missing pre-requisites for admission to the first year of university. It offers a Grade 12 bridging program and Year 1 of university. Graduates can then transfer into Year 2 at RMCC.

- **Canadian Forces College (CFC)**
  [www.cfc.forces.gc.ca]. Located in Toronto, CFC provides education in areas of defence, national security, operations and executive leadership. It also offers a Joint Command and Staff distance-learning program.

In addition to the above, the Military Personnel Generation Formation (MILPERSGEN), an umbrella educational organizing body, is responsible for the personnel-generating activities of the Canadian Armed Forces. This includes the Canadian

Defence Academy (CDA), the Leadership and Recruit School and support trade schools. Its mandate is to lead the CAF personnel-generating system in a manner that upholds distinction in the Profession of Arms.

The Army, Navy and Air Force oversee and ensure standards for their applicable-element training establishments. Training establishments specialize in the following:

- Aerospace studies (CF School of Aerospace Studies)
- Air Force selection (CF Aircrew Selection Centre) and international training
- Armoury
- Artillery
- Basic training for Regular Force Officers and non-commissioned members (CF Leadership and Recruit School)
- Chaplaincy
- Command (Canadian Army Command and Staff College)
- Communication
- Engineering
- Ethics
- Foreign military training
- Infantry
- Languages (CF Language School)
- Logistics
- Medical services
- Meteorology
- Military intelligence
- Military law (CF Military Law Centre)
- Military training abroad
- Peace support

- Pilot training (CF Flying Training School)
- Policing
- Public affairs
- Search and Rescue (CF School of Search and Rescue)
- Tactics

Leaving: Release from Military Service

Release or retirement from military service typically occurs after the member has completed their term of service, according to a Terms of Service (TOS) contract. However, releases can be granted prior to the end of the contract in some circumstances, if requested. The majority of releases are voluntary and approximately 15 percent are medically related. A minor percentage of releases are for dishonourable conduct or for having an unsatisfactory service record.

Terms of Service (TOS) start at three years but could be longer depending on the training required for a particular occupation. If the CAF pays for academic training at a civilian institution, the service member will be expected to serve an additional two months for each month of paid education.

Data collected from 2011 to 2014 indicates the average age of a CAF soldier at the time of release to be about 35 years overall and 43 years for medical releases.[27] So while the compulsory retirement age for CAF members is 55 (with an option to serve until age 60) it is noteworthy that those who join the CAF at the ages of 17 to 20 could have put in 20 years of military service and be "retiring" at the still relatively young age of 37 to 40.

⁕ ⁕ ⁕

Reservists

As noted previously, in addition to those who serve in the CAF Regular Forces, there is a CAF Reserve Force. One benefit of being a Reservist is the opportunity to work part-time for the CAF while developing skills for future employment without being tied to a long-term commitment. Many members of the Reserves hold full-time civilian jobs or attend school. Reservists work or receive training about four evenings and one weekend per month with their unit and are paid 85 percent of Regular Force salaries as well as a reasonable benefit package.

Unlike members of the Regular Forces, Reservists have the benefit of volunteering for deployments or training. However, in case of a national emergency (war or invasion) the Government of Canada can conscript them to serve full-time nationally or abroad.

In terms of civilian employment, the majority of Reservists may not have the same degree of difficulty transitioning since they never quite left the civilian world. Or if they did, their time away would have been shorter. Those (like Marc from our feature story on **page 105**) who served in a number of full-time contracts, however, might experience the same level of civilian adjustment and need as much support as their Regular Forces counterparts.

✳ ✳ ✳

Hopefully it is now clear that the military work environment is structured differently from most civilian workplaces. So then, what do we do to help our veteran clients find gainful employment? Before we get to that answer, Dick Gaither, president of Jobs Search Training Systems, Inc., suggests we ask our client a few basic questions:[28]

- Do you want to do exactly what you did in the military?

- Do you want to do something different?

- Are you interested in starting your own business?

- Do you want to go back to school?

- Do you want to take a break for a while or retire from the workforce?

The answers to all the above questions will help us determine our strategy.

KEY LEARNING

* Military culture is hierarchical. Respecting and adhering to the chain of command is expected of each soldier.

* A member's priority is first to the mission and last to self.

* To meet the requirements of deployability, a soldier must be mentally and physically fit.

* Competencies and qualities required to serve within the CAF are many and can be leveraged for civilian employment.

* Retirement from military service does not mean that one is old!

* Reservists may have different needs from Regular Force members.

PART II:
EMPLOYMENT AND
EMPLOYABILITY

Your goal should be to find a job that is [a] fit for you rather than one you think you might be able to fit into.

—Ron and Caryl Krannich[29]

"Bring actual skills to the table"

Emily, a professional engineer, is a corporal and has been a member of the CAF Reserve Force for over eight years. She has military roots: Her dad, uncle, and grandfather all served in the military. After high school Emily joined the reserves, following in the footsteps of a friend who had joined up the previous year.

Although Emily received many offers to go into full-time service, she prefers to remain part-time. She enjoys the carefree life of being a reservist. "All meals served, shacks to live in, lots of time for PT/gym, always people around to hang with/talk to." However, one of her not so favourite things is paperwork.

Emily now works full-time in the transportation division of a large company in British Columbia as a technical expert/advisor. She provides her team with the necessary procedural paperwork for the organization's transportation systems, helps to troubleshoot problems, advises on additional repairs and makes final calls on readiness of transports for release. She also provides parts as needed and ensures "stock is up to par at all times."

"Transition was easy," Emily says. "I've always had civilian engineering/technical jobs during my time in university.

Connections, proper resumé, military service and an engineering degree are what helped me get the job."

So what is Emily's advice?

"Prepare to work hard to first get that civilian job and then to keep it, especially in the present economy. Education is key.

"And lastly, but most importantly, bring actual skills that are required for that job/position to the table."

CHAPTER 3

The Big Picture: Veterans Face Unique Challenges

Much has been documented, especially to employer audiences, highlighting the qualities and skills former soldiers, sailors, airmen, and airwomen bring to the workplace. Employers are seeking candidates who, in addition to having job-specific skills, are adaptable, flexible, self-motivated, dependable, reliable, committed, professional, mission-focused and enthusiastic. According to CAF Transition Advisor Jo-Anne Flawn-LaForge, those who have been trained in military service possess these qualities and more:

- **Loyalty, dedication, and a sense of duty:** will stick with the task, no matter the hardship, until the mission is accomplished.

- **Teamwork/cooperation:** know how to work together for a common goal and trust each other to do what will ensure the success of the mission.

- **Leadership:** have been instructed in methods of managing, training, evaluating and developing staff; know how to have people follow you because they believe in you.

- **Problem solving:** have been trained to find the optimal solution to a problem and are prepared to discard a planned course of action as the situation changes, all while working under pressure and in circumstances where the stakes are extremely high.

- **Discipline:** have been trained to keep body and mind—everything from one's kit to personal grooming and mental and physical fitness—in top shape. Failure to do so might result in loss of the right to wear the uniform.

- **Knowledge of people:** know how to train, manage, command, and gain respect.

- **Goal orientation/Mission focus:** have been taught that the need of the mission overrides the need of the self.

- **Responsibility:** are responsible for the lives of others, expensive equipment or financial allocation.

- **Knowledge:** know how to operate communication systems and complex machinery, comply with safety standards, and pay attention to the smallest detail.

Given these more-than-stellar characteristics and skills, why do many experience difficulties finding and adjusting to new employment?

Lack of Knowledge About
Civilian Work Culture and Language

Those of us who advise clients on the logistics of navigating the civilian job market know that it can be challenging even for the savvy job seeker. That's why we offer individualized coaching, counselling or workshops to help clients learn the "tricks of the trade" and the language of the employer. We stress the importance of self-promotion, prepare our clients for behavioural and situational types of interview questions, and strongly advise them to do their market research.

Imagine then what it might be like for someone who for the past ten or fifteen years has lived in a completely different culture. In a very real sense, this is what it is like for servicemen and servicewomen who are transitioning to civilian careers. They experience a kind of culture shock.

As noted above and in the previous chapter, a military member's priority is first the mission, then the team, and finally the self. In civilian work culture, this is reversed. The civilian job seeker must point out to the prospective employer how he himself can help the organization achieve its mission or how she herself will add value to the organization. This requires a completely opposite mindset.

Our client is moving from a predominantly hierarchical, conforming environment with clearly defined roles and career progression to one that rewards self-promotion and self-reliance. By and large, civilian work culture tends to be more collaborative, allows for more role flexibility, has a less defined structure and career progression.[30]

A military member who is considering civilian employment must take time to understand the differences in the new work culture and the requirements needed to succeed. One former Officer interviewed for this guide said it this way: "If you don't know the environment you're transitioning to it's going to be problematic." Plain and simple!

A soldier would never go into a mission without doing the necessary reconnaissance, or "recce." The same is true when entering or re-entering the civilian workplace—especially after a long absence. Here are a few words from two veterans who I interviewed in 2014 for a CERIC report in response to the question "What was your biggest challenge in adjusting to civilian careers?":

> "I think my single biggest challenge was confidence that my abilities and skills would be translatable and appreciated by a civilian employer. I do not have a professional degree and was not employed in a readily transferable military occupation. As an Armoured Officer I was a leader and at times a manager, but I had to figure out both what I wanted to do and how my myriad of jobs over the years (most out of trade and without any training) would help me transition."

> "When I knew I was going to have to leave the Army I reached out to some of my more trusted connections and began asking them how they transitioned and how they choose their second career path. It was through these discussions with a few great people that I identified the skills and resources to guide my path."[31]

Not only is there a difference in work cultures, but there can also be a language barrier. Military speech can be hard to understand for those not used to it. Moreover, acronyms and initialisms abound in military language. If you notice this, don't shy away from asking your military client to provide translation using simple, non-military words. This might initially prove difficult for some but it is a necessary part of the transition. When you look at their resumé, you might find it too has to be "de-militarized." (More on this in the next chapter.)

It's our job to help our clients readjust their thinking so they can confidently describe, in language that's clear, how the culture of the military equipped them to be solid contributors to any organization.

Difficulty Articulating and Translating Skills

The how-to of translating military skills into civilian nomenclature and using this information to build stronger, more competitive resumés and cover letters is another area where career practitioners can assist the ex–military member. Start by asking simple questions:

• What skills did you use in this job?
• What did you need to do to complete a successful mission?

Sometimes clients have difficulty stepping back from what they've done for years to see and describe it objectively. When this happens, we could have them walk us through a typical day on the job, asking for details as they do so. As we listen, we take notes, documenting the skills we see at work. In working with former members of the military, especially those who worked in roles very different from any civilian equivalent, this "drawing out" process is critical. Another veteran interviewed in 2014 for the CERIC report said this:

> "Writing a resumé is foreign to those in the military. It's the employer/manager who makes the case for which employee is promoted. Vets are taught to be humble - (they) don't understand the need for elaborating on accomplishments and why it is important... Some coaching and mentorship in this area is useful."

So pull out those card sorts. Card-playing works especially well with clients who are more comfortable doing than speaking. Sorting Skills Cards can help clients see what they have done, what they want to continue doing or what they need to develop.

Sometimes, if a client is coming from a difficult job experience he may be feeling shaky about his skills. Maybe he was terminated or has been job searching for a while with little success. By now, self-doubt has crept in. Alternatively, if a client has been in combat, there is a high probability that her values might have shifted.[32] In these situations, instead of starting out with a skills-identification exercise, using Values Cards can be more effective.

Values are like the foundation of a house. They tell us about the things that anchor the client. Watch them and how they play the cards, then ask them to group the cards by theme. Based on your sense of the client, you can challenge some of their card placements, but mostly you want to see how their minds work. This knowledge helps us learn how to work with them. Finally, have them select 10 to 12 values that they want the next segment of their lives to comprise. It is amazing how telling this process can be—to them and to us.

Whether you start with Skills or with Values, this simple exercise (or any other self-assessment exercise you find useful) should help the ex-military member get at what they have to offer and the guiding principles that will undergird their choices.

Civilian Myths and Misperceptions

Myths about war and warfare abound. The life of a soldier—the work, training, military experiences and history—makes some people nervous.

Some employers admit that seeing on a resumé that a candidate has served a tour of duty in Afghanistan or Iraq gives them pause. Does she have a post-traumatic stress disorder? Will he require all kinds of accommodation on the job? Will she be a drain on resources? Other employers fear that if they hire veterans or those returning from a tour of duty, they might be called up again.

No one would argue that employers have an obligation to hire the best candidates to meet the workforce needs of their organizations. But according to management consultant Robert W. Goldfarb, "they also need to see each veteran as an individual, rather than as someone who might be bringing unwanted baggage back from the war."[33]

Assumptions and misperceptions persist however, affecting attitudes, beliefs and even hiring practices. One veteran I spoke with said that he and his peers often elect not to talk about their military careers except to those who've been through it.

How then do our clients tap into their vast military experience without making people nervous? While that question is on the floor, what happens when a veteran is no longer connected to a network of people with a shared past? Who do veterans talk to about what they did before returning to civilian life? These questions underscore the need for advocacy, raising awareness and veteran peer networks.

Advocacy

Veterans Affairs Canada, the CAF, Canada Company, and other organizations see educating employers about the benefits of hiring a former military members as a core part of their mission.

Raising awareness

Every year, on the first Sunday in June, Canada celebrates Canadian Armed Forces Day. In areas where there is a strong CAF presence, one typically finds more community partnerships and support. In large, urban settings the CAF presence is more diffuse. Remembrance Day events and activities continue to be meaningful in raising civilian awareness about the sacrifices of CAF members and veterans.

By treating each veteran as an individual, persisting in raising awareness and advocating on their behalf, much can be done to minimize the misperceptions that negatively impact hiring practices.

Not Knowing Civilian Job Equivalents

If the ex–military member has not done any pre-transition planning and has not sought out the assistance of any transition service professionals, and if his former military job was one for which there is no direct civilian equivalent, you can see how this might result in discouragement, unemployment or underemployment.

The client in the fictitious scenario described at the beginning of the book (see **page 18**) is an artillery soldier. These soldiers are responsible for conducting surveillance, locating targets and sending information to a command post. How then would you help this client find work? What civilian jobs do you think this person could do?

This is where a number of resources become useful, specifically

- the CAF's Military Occupations and Related Civilian Occupations table (see www.forces.gc.ca/en/business-reservist-support/tools-occupations.page);

- the CAF's Military to Civilian Trades table (see Appendix 1);

- the Veterans and Military Occupations Finder (VMOF), a listing of current US military occupations along with their civilian and Holland Code equivalents;[34] and

- "Information for Employers Hiring Veterans," a web page on the VAC website which links to position summaries for a number of military occupations (see www.veterans.gc.ca/eng/services/jobs/businesses-hiring-veterans). You can browse all CAF job descriptions here: www.forces.ca/en/jobexplorer/browsejobs-70.

From the Military to Civilian Trades table or the CAF job description, you will learn that one of the job equivalents for our artillery soldier is that of a computer network operator or a tractor trailer/heavy equipment operator.

A computer operator? A tractor trailer driver? How does the job of firing a gun get translated into these occupations?

Ask her! That's right. Ask the client to tell you what her job entailed. One recommendation from the literature encourages career practitioner to develop an open, honest relationship with our veteran clients. We should get them to teach us what they know.[35]

The operation of an artillery howitzer requires working with a team of seven people on several components to integrate information coming in from forward operatives. Our artillery soldier "operates technically advanced command-post computers, laser range-finders and fire-control computers."[36] In other words, information has to be fed into this equipment, targets set, the weapon fired, etc.—all very technical work. With this information you can now see how computer operator makes sense.

But what if our former artillery soldier is not interested in being a driver or computer operator?

Now we turn to a different resource: the Government of Canada's Job Bank (www.jobbank.gc.ca). Entering "artillery soldier" in the Job Bank brings up a list of related careers. This list includes occupations in correctional and protective services, areas that might be of greater interest to our client. Or we could use the VMOF, which for artillery soldier provides the two-letter Holland Code RI that opens up a wider range of occupational options related to the Realistic (R) or Investigative (I) types. How neat is that!

Research has shown a predominance of Realistic, Investigative, Enterprising and Social types in military occupations and personalities. Career practitioners are encouraged to become familiar with employment trends for those types so that when a veteran shows up at our door, we are armed with information.[37]

Lack of Knowledge About Services Available

While there is a wealth of services available to help CAF veterans, many of those interviewed for this project were not aware of them. An overview of the US literature from 2000 to 2013 supports this observation.[38] Vets reported little knowledge about

- services and supports available,

- transferability of skills,

- translating military skills to civilian occupations, and

- educational benefits.

Encourage transitioning members to keep connected with their VAC office (see www.veterans.gc.ca for locations). A guide to benefits available for CAF members, families and veterans is available online to help. Also, the VAC website has links to approved non-military service providers who can be of assistance.

❊ ❊ ❊

This completes the big-picture segment of Employment and Employability. Now let's get down to the nitty-gritty of what can be done to help our fictitious client address her employment needs.

KEY LEARNING

- ★ The CAF instils in members many skills that civilian employers need.

- ★ Misperceptions about the military affect civilian attitudes, beliefs and even hiring practices.

- ★ Resources are available to identify civilian equivalents to military jobs.

- ★ CAF members do not always know about the services available to help them in the transition to civilian life.

YVONNE'S FAVOURITES

The **Government of Canada Job Bank** *includes a skills and knowledge checklist whereby job seekers can identify their skills from 10 categories and their knowledge from nine areas. Results yield a Skills and Knowledge Profile showing related occupations, skills matches and knowledge needed. By clicking on the occupations, one can view all the current jobs available by region.*

The **Veterans and Military Occupations Finder** *(VMOF), though not a Canadian resource, can help career practitioners and CAF veterans identify civilian equivalents to military occupations. The two-letter Holland Code identifier is particularly useful in generating additional career options. Use with the caveat that US military occupations do not always match CAF occupations directly.*

The business of transitioning from the military to a civilian occupation is the business of decisions.

—Dick Gaither,
"Military Transition Management"[39]

"A new chapter"

Natalie joined the Canadian Armed Forces immediately out of high school. What made her decide to join? "A sense of duty and service to my country [and] a sense of adventure." Plus, living in a small prairie town did not provide many options for full-time, gainful employment.

Her 14 years of military service were all in the Regular Forces. The first five years she worked as an administrative clerk, starting as a Non-commissioned Private then as a Corporal, and the next nine years as a Logistics Officer. By the time she left, she had attained the rank of Captain.

The decision to leave the CAF was primarily for family reasons. Her spouse, "a 20-year veteran, was medically released following the diagnosis of an inoperable traumatic brain injury (TBI) while serving in Afghanistan. After his release, he found employment in Toronto."

Says Natalie: "In order to ensure our family remained together and we were financially stable, we decided to relocate to Toronto. My release ensured we would remain together as a family unit. [Plus] I was also looking for a new challenge outside of the military so we could move forward with a new chapter in our lives."

When asked what she misses most she has a long list: the routine, the camaraderie, the confidence her supervisors had in her ability to tackle any problem, being the go-to person. "I miss providing advice, [and] guiding and mentoring those that were part of my team."

Her next comment made me chuckle. "I also miss wearing army boots as my daily footwear (seriously, high heels really hurt!)"

For Natalie, transitioning out of uniform was initially stressful and a source of anxiety. "I left without so much as having a CV completed and had misconceptions about how easy it would be to enter the workforce, especially in Toronto. While I have 14 years of proven experience, I have had to step back, [to] take time to really adjust my language in order to communicate in civilian speak what I have done, how it can relate to their organizations and why I am value added."

Networks are also important. "Having a limited network initially also was difficult because it did not allow me to reach out as quickly as I had hoped."

So what was the turning point?

"The turning point for me was finding a mentor who really pushed me, was brutally honest about the things I needed to do, and was able to provide advice throughout every step of my transition."

Anything else?

"Interfacing with Canada Company was extremely helpful because it helped bridge the gap between military and civilian employment by connecting me to contacts supportive of military veterans, by assisting with my CV, and by acting as a sounding board to get me thinking about my skill sets and what fields I should be looking at."

What was most challenging for Natalie during this process?

"The most difficult thing has been to turn myself into a salesperson to effectively market myself and not to undersell my skills."

Natalie has come to appreciate that there are "many similarities between the military and some of the bigger organizations, such as challenges in culture, hierarchies, the requirement to provide support."

She sees how many of the skills and attributes learned in the military can be put to use within the civilian job market. "Our ability to think on the fly, provide direction, communicate effectively, prioritize and manage stressful situations."

I asked her what advice she would give to a CAF member who is about to make the transition to civilian life. Her detailed response was as follows (emphasis added):

"Take time to do a lot of **research**. Know where you want to go, the skills that you need to have, and have real examples of what you have done so you can assist your potential future employer in determining how you will fit into their organization.

"For instance, creating **STAR stories** (describing the Situation, identifying the Task, what Action you took, and the Result you achieved) will help you AND the employer demonstrate the skills you have. It will also help you become more confident in what you have done and bring that confidence when you meet with people.

"Attempt to **de-militarize** how you speak and communicate. Jargon is only applicable to those in the organization and it is more of a barrier when you are trying to convince others that you belong in their organization

"**Network** long before you decide to leave. Take people out for coffee to learn about them and what they do; do not start sniffing around for a job immediately but take the time to grow your network since this is what will assist in finding gainful employment when you are ready. Talk to people who have already transitioned, link up with companies, such as Canada Company, who have helped people transition. They are a wealth of knowledge and information and will be able to steer you in the right direction.

"Finally, **be realistic** in your timelines. Ensure you do your time appreciation/estimate and work backwards so you know what you need to do before you jump. It will be less stress when you are ready to transition out of uniform."

At the time of this writing, Natalie is still exploring where in the private sector she will best fit. She is taking time to walk the talk—network, research, upgrade her education and enhance her skills.

CHAPTER 4

Employment and Employability: Tools, Services and Jobs

Richard N. Bolles, author of *What Color Is Your Parachute?*, emphatically asserts that the number one need of returning veterans is to find a job.[40] He calls for more career practitioners who are adept at the "mechanics of career development" (step-by-step guidance), to take on this most important task in supporting our veterans.

Mechanics fix that which is no longer working or not working well. So how can we as career practitioners employ our "mechanical" skills to help the veteran client? What do veterans need from us?

Veterans interviewed for this project were asked this question. This is what they identified:

1. Programs like the one offered by Canada Company
2. Access to employers
3. Job banks
4. Placement/Job fairs
5. Online network forums
6. Assessment of what I can do and how/ where to target my research
7. Resumé help
8. Resumé samples
9. "You are here" flowchart and where I fit in the process
10. List of skills
11. Civilian job equivalents
12. Online questionnaire to help veterans identify needs and link to services available
13. One-on-one coaching
14. Online tools
15. List of resources to help veterans
16. Second-career workshops
17. Integration of existing resources
18. Job search assistance

19. Webinars
20. Lessons learned from those who have transitioned from the military
21. Credentialing
22. "Someone who is going to help me through the process," meaning personalized one-on-one services

Quite a list, isn't it? What these interviewees are asking for to assist with employment matches the findings and recommendations of research. Compare the list above to this one:

1. Job finding information and tools specific to veterans
2. Information on civilian/military job equivalencies
3. Career practitioners dedicated to helping veterans find work
4. How to overcome obstacles to employment
5. Constructing civilian resumés; list of professional coaching and writing services
6. Career fairs and access to job listings
7. Translation of military skills/jobs into civilian-workplace language
8. Tools for assessing transferable skills
9. Online and paper resources
10. Trends in occupations for which released soldiers have previous training
11. Case stories from employers

Tooling Your Client for the Job Search Process

Here we will examine a few of the tools that our veteran clients will need in order to secure a job: skills, an effective resumé, job leads, and interview preparation.

Transferable Skills[41]

In preparing a transitioning military client for the job of finding employment, we would agree that skills assessment is an important step—a necessary component of the "tooling" process. For the artillery soldier in our fictitious scenario (see Introduction, **page 18**), the challenge might be in identifying which of her skills are relevant to the type of civilian work she wants to do. By having the client perform a transferability skills checklist, or by using your favourite skills-assessment exercise, you will ensure she not only knows what she has to offer, but can also clearly articulate and illustrate her skills during a job interview (more on that to come). Remember, the CAF provides excellent training in skills that are transferable to the civilian workplace, in three areas:

- **Technical:** Skills learned in one's trade or profession
- **Leadership:** How to command, lead, guide and mentor
- **Interpersonal:** Working as part of a team

Veterans also demonstrate these valued qualities: responsibility, reliability, and a "get it done" attitude.

The Resumé: From "Militarized" to "De-militarized"

Let's see what a militarized resumé might look like and how to fix it. The sample on **pages 84-85** is based on the resumé of a real CAF veteran. Here are a few problems and areas in need of work:

- **Lack of career objective:** Resumés should clearly state the type of work sought or the skills the candidate wants to use in employment.

- **Use of military acronyms/language:** What is IBEW local? Unit 4 Watch supervisor? Petty Officer?

- **Missing information:** Where did this candidate work? Locations for some positions have not been included.

- **Formatting:** The use of fonts and layout could be improved.

For the most part, this resumé documents what Douglas Sample did without highlighting the components of his experience he'd like to use in future employment.

Now compare this resumé to the revised version on **pages 86-87**. Do you see how the problems listed above have been addressed? What other improvements do you notice?

DOUGLAS SAMPLE

154 xxxxxxxxxx, Hamilton, ON L8K 2V4   905-XXX-XXXX   xxxxx@hotmail.com

PROFESSIONAL EXPERIENCE

IEC Electric   **September 2014 – February 2015**
Solar Farm Fabrication Technician   *(through IBEW local)*
Working in a team environment ensuring electrical wiring is placed correctly within the 1000 acre solar farm facility. Motivating team members in harsh weather conditions.
Performing fitness co-ordinator duties for morning stretches before going into the field.
First aid responder for team members if required. Meeting daily targets and company goals.
Recently asked to supervise 12 new hires for training. Took on duties of team bus driver as requested from foreman to ensure safe arrival and departure of colleagues to and from construction areas.

H.B.White Electric   **February 2014 – June 2014**
Solar Farm Fabrication Technician   *(through IBEW local)*
Working in a team environment constructing a 100 acre Solar farm from start to finish in extreme weather conditions at times. Trouble shooting technical problems and anticipating tasking priorities to achieve daily and weekly targets.

Black and McDonald Electric   **December 2012 to February 2013**
                                                     (through IBEW loc 105)
Employed as a permit worker within the union. Assigned to QA/QC team rapidly. My work ethic was observed and complemented by co-workers and various foremen on numerous occasions.

Canadian Forces Recruiting Centre   **October 2001 to September 2012**
Hamilton
Recruiter
Supervised and evaluated 9 recruiters within their particular geographical areas of responsibility in Southern Ontario through Personnel Evaluation Reports (PERs). Produced working schedules and provided positive feedback as well as disciplinary measures as required.
Provided information on all aspects of the Canadian Forces to potential applicants for enrolment during contact interviews. Developed and delivered current presentations for schools, job fairs, etc.
Over 450 presentations to date. Maintained confidential personnel files during the recruiting process to achieve entry into the Canadian Forces. Conducted telephone background reference checks on Canadian Forces applicants. Attended many conferences, workshops and community events across Canada for augmentation or brain storming sessions to improve the recruiting process for applicants to the CF.

DOUGLAS SAMPLE

154 xxxxxxxxxx, Hamilton, ON L8K 2V4   905-XXX-XXXX   xxxxx@hotmail.com

Environmental Sciences Group   **February 1993 to July 2001**
The Royal Military College of Canada
Purchasing and Logistics Co-ordinator
Researched, planned, organized and deployed numerous field research teams to sites across
Canada, mainly in remote areas of the Arctic region and research vessel deployments.
Supervised an "Operations Centre" procuring all equipment, flights, charters, lodgings, cash
advances and claims, for many science teams in the field. I facilitated all procurement of
equipment for home offices as well as research groups at the University of British Columbia as
well as a department of Queen's University in Kingston, ON.
Maintained inventory and accounting for a multi-million dollar company. Proficient with MS
Excel, MS Word, MS Access, and MS Powerpoint. Assisted with sampling programs in remote
areas on land and at sea. Marine survey team leader.

Royal Canadian Naval Reserve   **June 1983 to Present**
Various Units across Canada
Petty Officer 1st Class Boatswain
Harbour Defence Unit 4 watch supervisor. Manned exercises across the country with personnel
from 24 units. Instructed Drill & seamanship, qualified as a range safety officer, small boat
coxswain, shipboard petty officer, fire leader, rescue team leader, spill response team member,
supervisor of daily routine & evolutions on board ship. Chief and Petty Officer's mess bar
manager and vice president (volunteer).

EDUCATION
Mohawk College of Applied Arts and Technology. Hamilton, ON
Law & Security, General Business   September 1983 to April 1986

PROFESSIONAL DEVELOPMENT
- Instructor for classroom and practical military operations
- St John's Ambulance Basic First Aid and CPR
- Fire warden for office and warehouse buildings
- Petty Officer of the year, HMCS Cataraqui, Kingston, ON
- Safe driving / backing certification
- Rescue boat driver, regattas, air shows, search & rescue tactics
- Restricted Operator's Certificate of Proficiency in Radio
- Professional sales training program certified – Salesforce Training & Consulting inc.
- Senior Leadership Qualified
- Canadian Decoration 2nd Clasp
- Commander's Commendation Award for facilitating and co-ordinating Remembrance Day
  Ceremonies and Canadian Football League Forces Appreciation Game.

Sample resumé, de-militarized

DOUGLAS SAMPLE

154 xxxxxxxxxx, Hamilton, ON L8K 2V4   905-XXX-XXXX   xxxxxx@hotmail.com
https://ca.linkedin.com/pub/doug-xxxxx/2x/4xx/XXa

PROFILE

I transform companies by my distinguished career in the Canadian Forces, capitalizing on operational planning, team leadership, conflict resolution training and coaching staff.

PROFESSIONAL EXPERIENCE

IEC Electric, Cayuga, ON   2014 – 2015
Solar Farm Fabrication Technician
- **Increased morale** by motivating 10+ team members in harsh weather conditions
- Installed electrical wiring on a team of 20 within a 1,000–acre solar farm facility
- Served as fitness co-ordinator and First aid responder for team members
- Selected to supervise 12 new hires for training.
- Chosen by foreman to act as team bus driver to construction sites

H. B. White Electric, Welland, ON   2014
Solar Farm Fabrication Technician
- **Exceeded daily targets** and company goals by 2% through troubleshooting technical problems and prioritizing
- Constructed a 100–acre solar farm on a team of 15, from start to finish, in adverse climates   .

Black and McDonald Electric, Hagersville, ON   2012 – 2013
Solar Farm Fabrication Technician
- Promoted to Quality Assurance/Quality Control team rapidly
- Praised by co-workers and 3 foremen for strong work ethic

Canadian Forces Recruiting Centre, Hamilton, ON   2001 – 2012
Recruiter
- Supervised and evaluated 9 recruiters within Ontario through personnel evaluation reports. Provided positive feedback to encourage staff's performance
- Promoted 100+ career opportunities and interviewed potential applicants for enrollment
- Boosted the reputation and brand of the Canadian Forces F by developing and delivering 450+ presentations at schools and job fairs

Environmental Sciences Group   1993 – 2001
The Royal Military College of Canada
Purchasing and Logistics Co-ordinator
- Marine survey team leader. Organized 2 field teams to sites across Canada, mainly in the Arctic, to research vessel deployments.
- Supervised an "Operations Centre" arranging all equipment, flights, charters, lodgings, cash advances and claims. Maintained $50k+ inventory and accounting for a multi-million dollar company

DOUGLAS SAMPLE

905-XXX-XXXX   xxxxxx@hotmail.com   https://ca.linkedin.com/pub/doug-xxxxx/2x/4xx/XXa

PROFESSIONAL EXPERIENCE (Cont'd)

Royal Canadian Naval Reserve   1983 – present
Various Units across Canada
Petty Officer

- Supervised Harbour Defence operations across the country with personnel from 24 departments.
- Led daily operations onboard ship: instructed Drill & seamanship, qualified as a range safety officer, fire leader, rescue team leader, environment team member
- Served as Bar Manager and Vice-President, Chief and Petty Officer's mess

EDUCATION

Diploma, Mohawk College of Applied Arts and Technology, Hamilton, ON
Concentration: Law & Security, General Business
GPA 3.5

PROFESSIONAL DEVELOPMENT/CERTIFICATIONS

- Basic First Aid and CPR courses – St John's Ambulance
- Unit environmental officer certification – Canadian Forces
- Fire warden for office and warehouse buildings
- Safe driving certification
- Courses in rescue boat driving, regattas, air shows, search & rescue tactics
- Restricted Operator's Certificate of Proficiency in Radio
- Smart Serve certification
- Professional sales training program certified – Salesforce Training & Consulting inc.
- Health and safety representative – Canadian Forces

ACHIEVEMENTS

- Petty Officer of the year, HMCS Cataraqui, CFB Kingston, ON
- Decoration medal for years served in the Canadian Forces
- Commander's Commendation Award, facilitating and co-ordinating Remembrance Day Ceremonies and Canadian Football League Forces Appreciation Game

Educator and author Randall Hansen offers the following resumé tips to military job seekers:[42]

- Clarify your job objective
- Target the resumé to address employer needs
- Do not include combat details
- Assume the reader has no knowledge of the military
- Showcase how the military equipped you
  with skills (technical, leadership, problem-
  solving, interpersonal, etc.)
- Highlight core values, accomplishments
  and areas of expertise
- Seek feedback on your resumé draft
  and adjust it accordingly.

The addition of a key words section or a skills summary would help flag areas of expertise so that when hiring managers search their applications databases, this applicant would pop up in the list of potentially suitable candidates. Targeting the resumé language to reflect exactly the skills, experiences, education or certifications the employer is looking for is also good practice.

Case in point: I once had a staff member give notice to leave her job during an especially busy time for my department. I needed to post and fill the job ASAP. The day following the application deadline, when I went to check the applicant pool, I discovered over 400 resumés for the one position. No one, myself included, wants to go through such a daunting task, plus I definitely did not have the time. So what I did was use a series of filters to flag only the resumés that met all of the job requirements.

Finally, applicants should demonstrate that they are connected and current with social media. In the revised sample resumé, notice the addition of the direct link to Douglas's LinkedIn profile.

These are examples of small but important tips career practitioners can offer to help transitioning military members ensure their resumés are civilian-workplace ready.[43]

Jobs Leads

Job training services, links to military-friendly employers, online networks, retraining subsidies, job listings, transition planning, resumé and job search help are available to transitioning members and veterans. Some of these services can be accessed before one leaves the military so that adequate preplanning can be done. For easy reference, here are a few that focuses on employment and career services:

CAF Career Transition Services

Whether one has reached retirement age or is planning to leave the CAF after a shorter period of service, the CAF Career Transition Services are the most likely place to seek assistance. This service is available to Regular and Reserve Force members as well as survivors of a CAF member and provides information on benefits and tools one needs to transition to civilian life and careers. These services are provided on every CAF base/ wing through the Personnel Selection Offices (PSO).

- **Second Career Assistance Network (SCAN):** Through seminars, members can learn about the benefits and services available to them and their families as they prepare to leave the military.

- **Career Transition Workshops (CTW):** Through the PSO, transitioning members can attend workshops that cover resumé writing, self-assessment, job search and interview skills.

- **Counselling Services** are available through the PSO. Services include career and education counselling, career assessment and career search software, and interest inventories.

Veterans Affairs Canada (VAC)

VAC works jointly with CAF to offer a number of programs for members desiring civilian employment after their military careers. They actively seek partnerships with private sector employers to advance the case for employing veterans.

VAC Career Transition Services: Effective the day after the date of release and for up to two years after, members can receive reimbursements for services accessed through service providers for the following:

- career assessment
- aptitude testing
- job search
- resumé writing
- interview assistance
- career counselling
- services of a recruiting agent

Transition interviews: Cross-Canada service teams work with military personnel to determine in advance the needs for them and their family prior to leaving military service and will advise and help set up supports.

Vocational and rehabilitation assistance: In addition to medical and psychosocial assistance, vocational services help members identify suitable careers, provide some financial assistance if additional training is required, and assist with job finding.

Both **CAF Transition Services** and **VAC** partner with non-military service providers such as Canada Company, Helmets to Hardhats, and Prince's Operation Entrepreneur (more on these below) to help members secure civilian employment and careers. Through this program, they

- promote to employer the skills/competencies/ attributes of military staff;

- provide information on military ranks, job descriptions and (for some) recommendations on civilian equivalents.

Veterans Hiring Act (Jobs with the Federal Government)

Up to five years post release, honourably released CAF members who have served a minimum of three years are eligible to apply for internal postings in the federal public service.

Medically released members may qualify for regulatory or statutory priority hiring status. Priority status can be activated up to five years from date of release and is in effect for five years. The member must meet all requirements of the position and must be certified as able to return to work.

Members deemed through VAC to have a service-related injury or illness receive statutory priority, which is the highest level of priority status.[44]

Canada Company Military Employment Transition (MET) Program [www.canadacompany.ca]

Next to the CAF and VAC Career Transition Services, the MET Program is highly recommended for any transitioning military personnel with whom you are working. MET is a partnership between Canada Company, Canadian Armed Forces and Veterans Affairs Canada. Not only does it offer employment services for CAF members who have been honourably released, it also partners with employers and other related service providers to do so.

Upon registration, CAF members and veterans can access these resources:

- A job search flowchart which helps job seekers identify where they are on the employment landscape and what they need to do

- Videos on different aspects of career assessment and the job search process. Includes resumé, cover letter and reference templates; military ranks with civilian equivalents; interview and self-promotion tips; and LinkedIn information

- 165+ military-friendly employers

- Job listings directly from organizations

- Entrepreneurial opportunities

- Access to E-mentors—HR and other career professionals who volunteer their time to help members with resumés, cover letters, interviews, salary information and jobs

Employers can learn about these aspects of the military:

- Military culture and system

- Military ranks and civilian job equivalents

- Military trades and civilian job equivalents

- Skills, attributes and competencies of CAF members

**Forces@WORK [www.forcesatwork.ca] and
Base To Business [www.vetyournexthire.com]**

Both of these programs are offered through Prospect Human Resources in Alberta. Forces@WORK provides the following services for transitioning military personnel:

- Direct placement, employment and labour market tools

- Skills transferability, resumé and interview preparation

- Supports in areas of retention and cultural transition

- Personalized case management

- Access to assistive technologies

- Assistance in understanding employment-related military benefits

The Base To Business program offers consultative services to employers to assist them in understanding the culture of the military so they can be better equipped to provide a welcoming and accommodating work environment for new hires.

Helmets to Hardhats (H2H) [www.helmetstohardhats.ca]

This is a partnership with building-trade unions, associations and government for those interested in a career in the building and construction industry.

- Offers assistance in finding apprenticeships to achieve journeyperson qualifications in building and construction trades as well as management positions in this industry.

- Provides assistance with resumés.

Prince's Operation Entrepreneur [www.princesoperationentrepreneur.ca]

Operated through Prince's Charities Canada, this program is specifically for transitioning military members and veterans interested in starting their own business. It offers:

- Seven-day boot camps: Participants must already have a well thought-out business idea. They receive training in business planning, marketing, and accounting.

- One-day workshops: Provide an introduction to entrepreneurship to CAF members, veterans and spouses.

- Mentoring and financing through the Futurpreneur program: Up to $15,000 for qualifying applicants of any age and up to $30,000 through the Business Development Triple-Up Program for qualified applicants 39 years old or younger.

- Networking opportunities through webinars and an entrepreneur-in-residence.

Canadian Franchise Association's Military Veteran's Program

The Canadian Franchise Association offer special discounts, incentives and employment opportunities for honourably released military members who are interested in franchising or working in a franchise. The CFA's position is that the discipline, leadership, commitment and ability to work within a "standard operating procedure" are qualities veterans have that fit the franchise model. Those interested can log in via the Canada Company website or go to http://lookforafranchise.ca/cfa-military-veterans-program/.

Career Edge Internship Program for CAF Reservists

This new program recently announced by the federal government "helps Reservists overcome barriers to employment through paid internships that provide coaching and the knowledge required to successfully transition to the civilian labour force."[45] A subsidized paid internship is open to young reservists between the ages of 19 and 30 who have at least a high school diploma and have not previously participated in any Career Edge Internships. The program began in August 2015, with 50 reservists to be placed in internships during year 1, 75 in year 2 and 100 in year 3 for a total of 225 placements. Assisted placement into unsubsidized paid internships is available to reservists and veterans not in the specified age range.

Other

The **10,000 Jobs Coalition:** In 2012, Canada Company, through its MET Program partners, challenged corporate Canada to hire 10,000 CAF veterans by 2023. More than 100 employers are committed to making this initiative a success. The 10,000 Jobs Coalition is on target and to date has hired a total of 1,081 CAF members and veterans. At the time of this writing, the MET Program has over 4,300 registered military members from across Canada and over 165 military-friendly employer participants.

Employer participants represent a range of industries: banking, finance, manufacturing, business services, food services, telecommunications, government and security. You can see the complete list of these veteran-friendly employers at www.canadacompany.ca/canadacompany/met/en/military-members-and-veterans/military-friendly-employers/index.jsp.

Kijiji Support our Troops Initiative: Employers advertising on Kijiji who are interested in hiring veterans have a yellow Veteran Friendly ribbon beside their ads. Once you've logged on to the Kijiji job site, select "veteran friendly" from the Featured Ads menu listing to view these employers.

LinkedIn groups: Hire Canadian Military, Military Employment Transition and Canadian Veterans in Business are closed groups on LinkedIn where employers will also post positions to veteran members.

The Interview

All we career practitioners have within our toolkits tried and proven interview tips. In addition to the pre-interview basics — research the organization, ensure the resumé is job ready, line up references, choose appropriate attire — the novice veteran job searcher will likely require more than one interview prep session. Because they come from a work culture where performance and seniority form the basis for promotions, where promotions are initiated at the recommendation of one's commanding officer, and where self-promotion is not a core value, veterans are understandably not used to or even comfortable with the idea of selling themselves.

Without trying to tell career professionals like you how to do your job, I present these questions for our mutual consideration:

- How will we prepare our clients to address employer skepticism about their ability (or willingness) to adapt to a civilian work culture?

- How will we teach our clients to speak knowledgeably about the added value they bring to an organization?

- What tips will we offer to help them describe how their military background has equipped them with skills that can meet an employer's needs? What would we do, for example, to encourage a veteran client to describe the scope of his responsibility when at a young age he might have managed a number of people or a budget far exceeding that of a similar-aged civilian counterpart?

- How will we do these things with a client who has been steeped in a culture of "self last, mission first"?

Suggestions for Practitioners

As you can see, there is a range of employment services and initiatives available to veterans. Sometimes, however, in the course of our work with a particular client group we discover a missing component or a gap. If that's the case, partner with an existing military-oriented service provider where possible to bring that added component to fruition instead of trying to create yet one more separate resource for veterans to discover.

What is not so readily available are career practitioners across Canada versed in and adept at working with transitioning military members. If you recall, on the list of needs at the beginning of this chapter, transitioning military members interviewed wanted "someone to help me through the process."

It is the personal touch, the one-to-one service, the step-by-step guidance that is needed and treasured. With that in mind, and in keeping with the needs identified at the beginning of this chapter, permit me to offer a few suggestions:

- Have your military clients register with Canada Company's MET Program and/or other complementary services that will support them in their search for work. MET offers job listings, job equivalence tools, and access to employers.

- Focus on helping your clients identify the skills, personal attributes, values and experiences that will help them land a job.

- Follow through on Bolles' recommendation by providing a step-by-step guide to finding work. Offer practical instructions, for example: "You are here. Where do you want to go? How can I help you get there?"

- Offer workshops or webinars if you have a critical mass.

- Provide hands-on, customized and individualized career coaching/counselling tailored to meet the unique needs of your military client. Each is different.

- For those clients wanting to go deep, *and if you are professionally trained in counselling,* employ some of the strategies discussed in Chapter 5 to help them get to a place of job readiness.

- Get to know the resources that are available to assist with support, training, education and employment.

- Learn which organizations are veteran friendly.

- Form a coalition or join a coalition of career practitioners who can share information as well as best practices in working with transitioning military members.

- Attend or inquire about events, job fairs, conferences, workshops or activities for transitioning military members to keep your knowledge up-to-date.

Working with Reservists: Military Leave

The number of Reservists who are being deployed has grown in recent years. In addition to their part-time employment as members of the CAF Reserve Force, many Reservists are employed in civilian jobs while some are students. Reservists can also volunteer to participate in operations thus changing from part-time to full-time service.

To provide protection for Reservists working in civilian jobs or attending academic institutions, in 2012 all the provinces and territories in association with the federal government passed Job Protection Legislation for Reservists.[46] The Legislation stipulates what employers must do when granting leave to deploying Reservists.

While the details of the legislation might differ for each provincial or territorial jurisdiction, all military leave policies have the following in common: all reservist leave is unpaid, requires a minimum qualification period, and must stipulate the frequency and length of the leave of absence. The legislation protects Reservists after they return from deployment or from an extended period of military training.

If you have any clients who are serving in the Reserve Force, here are some useful tips to share with them:

- There is no need to quit your job to serve on deployment.

- Make sure you are prepared when approaching employers with a request for leave.

- Comply with the requirements set out by your employer. Employer policies for a leave-of-absence request's notice period can range from one to three months.

- Sample letters can be found on the CAF website.[47]

- Find out if you will be returning to the same job or an equivalent.

- (For students) Check your institution's policy regarding delaying the completion of your program of study.

We are now more aware of the military-to-civilian-employment landscape. What we have not yet addressed—and need to, based on experience—is the reality that even though our clients may be anxious to find meaningful work,48 for some, additional factors like the need for further education/training, mental challenges, or physical challenges stand between them and their desired goal.

We also know we are not equipped to be all things to all people. That's why we keep as current as we can on programs, service providers, initiatives, tools and strategies. Our knowledge is one of our best commodities.

Next let's explore some fairly simple things we can do to help clients overcome transitional barriers to employment.

* Transitioning military clients want practical, hands-on information and one-on-one, step-by-step help.

* A number of career and employment programs and services are available to help transitioning veterans look for and find work in different occupational areas.

* Career practitioners should become familiar with what's out there; complement, not duplicate, available resources; join a career practitioner forum.

YVONNE'S FAVOURITES

Military to Civvie Street, *an e-book written by Audrey Prenzel, provides succinct information on how to de-militarize a resumé and many resumé samples. This resource is Canadian.*[49]

PART III:
PRE-EMPLOYMENT
READINESS

Photo credit: Canadian Forces Combat Camera, DND

Transitions are more important than chronological age for understanding and evaluating an individual's behavior.

—Anderson, et al.,
Counseling Adults in Transition[50]

"Trying to find my way"

Marc served in the CAF for 39 years as a member of the Reserve Forces. Eighteen of those 39 years he served full-time in a number of contract roles that would last anywhere from one to three years. He served twice in Afghanistan and once in Kosovo.

Because of his many years of service, Marc was eligible to receive retirement benefits in 2013 but due to the part-time and contractual nature of his tenure, he finds he does not have enough to live on.

It was the need for a summer job that initially prompted Marc to join the CAF. His primary job was that of a military engineer and at the time of his retirement he had the rank of Lieutenant-Colonel.

He misses the "challenge, helping people who need help across the world, and being a mentor." He misses his rank of Lieutenant-Colonel. "I am now nobody."

His biggest challenge on retirement from the CAF was what to do. Marc feels he's still young and has something to offer. He was not prepared for his transition. He had no idea what to do in his post-military career, or the skills and credentials that would be recognized when he "got out." He had no contacts or networks within the civilian world. While he had managed a number of big engineering projects in the CAF, he does not have an engineering degree—something he needs if he wants to do similar work in the civilian job market.

His advice to someone who is transitioning from military to civilian employment is that now is too late. "This is something that needs to be prepared in advance."

Right now, Marc is "trying to find my way. Maybe go in the arts world (painting, woodworking, drawing, sculpture)."

CHAPTER 5

Enhancing Coping and Adaptation: Strategies and Support Networks

Clients seeking our professional assistance are not always clear about what they want from us or what they want us to do for them. We can help them by providing information to increase their self-knowledge, information about career options, guidance in decision making, and assessment of their career readiness. Do not hesitate to ask them why they've come to seek your services. What do they hope you can do for them? Why now? What prompted them to book an appointment?

Asking questions like these allows us to hear and determine if we are the appropriate "solution" for their need. Sometimes we're not.

Assessment

Once we have outlined our approach to career decision-making and the client has determined that what we offer will meet their needs, the real work begins. In the 2014 Veterans issue of the *Career Planning and Adult Development Journal*, Robert Miles offers some suggestions we can employ in our work with transitioning military clients or veterans:[51]

Assess career decision-making readiness: Next to employment, the other pressing need of the veteran is overcoming barriers. Some of these barriers are personal—a result of mental health or physical injuries. Some are systemic or societal. Is the client ready to proceed with career decision-making?

Assess interests and options: What are the motivators for this client? Through interest inventories, storytelling or other tools, the client can evaluate activities in their military occupations or leisure pursuits that they enjoyed and begin to see energizing possibilities.

Assess skills: Helping veteran clients determine the importance of their motivated skills (high interest + high proficiency) as opposed to their unmotivated skills (low interest + high proficiency) will help them design effective resumés and prepare for job interviews.

Assess changes in values: Sometimes military service can have a drastic impact on the veteran's values. Sorting easy-to-manipulate Values Cards can allow them to compare how and what values have shifted, from then to now. Sometimes the shift means a change in their worldview. For example, "recognition" or "status" used to mean a lot. Now the focus might be on "security" or "stability." This provides an opportunity for the veteran to vocalize feelings or thoughts and provides us with useful information on their core priorities.

Assist in decision making: Career practitioners can help clients separate short-term from long-term goals. What are factors for immediate consideration? Family issues, financial challenges, education? Helping clients sift through and determine their most pressing priorities at this stage is so very important.

Assist in implementation: Often this is where we lose our clients and where they need the most support. During the assessment phase or career counselling, clients are, for the most part, recipients of information. We provide them with results from whatever battery of inventories we have asked them to complete and help them see patterns and possibilities. At this implementation juncture, however, the client must take action. The proverbial ball is back in his court. (That's why determining readiness is such a critical step.)

For the client whose immediate priority is to find employment, the next step is active job searching. That means lots of networking, informational interviews, attending job fairs, facing possible rejection and employer biases, and keeping one's spirits up. Similarly, those who have opted for further education or training can benefit from our expertise in helping them navigate the landscape of civilian education— applications, credit transfers, accommodation (if needed), course selection, financial aid, and so on.

Strategies/Approaches for Counselling Veterans

Let's take a look at a few approaches/strategies that can be both effective and relevant when working with veteran clients.[52]

Transition Planning — Schlossberg's 4-S Model

Faced with the pressing need to find a job or get an education, the "new" veteran may not take time—or see the need to take time—to come to terms with the past before launching into the future. However, events (like leaving the CAF) and non-events (the expectation of something that never materializes) are both life changing, and changes are transitions. This is why Mary Anderson and Jane Goodman recommend Schlossberg's 4-S Model for working with veterans as they move through the transition process.[53]

This model, which focuses on Situation, Self, Support and Strategies, can help practitioners plan interventions in line with the client's strengths and liabilities to enhance their coping and adaptation, especially as they move from a work system that was hierarchical and conforming to one that is focused on self-reliance and self-promotion.

The **Situation** question—"What is happening now?"—gives the transitioning member a chance to take stock. Answers can vary widely: "I'm leaving the military after ___ [number of] years," " I am injured," "My family dynamics have changed," "I am not sure what job I can get."

The **Self** question—"How am I perceiving myself during this transition?"—can also be framed as "How am I really doing?" This allows the client to examine his or her feelings.

Fear? Excitement? Anxiety? Our personal and psychological resources—values, spirituality, resilience and life outlook—come into play every time we are challenged by changes.

Support is so important as people make life transitions. This is particularly apt for transitioning military members. They need the support of family, friends, networks, employers, career professionals and peers. They need a space or place to speak honestly and receive affirmation, feedback and assistance. Key questions: "What supports do I have?" "What supports do I need?"

Strategies: "How do I typically cope with change?" "What mechanisms do I use to help me prepare for the unexpected?" Coping strategies help us to control the impact or meaning of a problem, modify the situation and manage stress. Individuals cope best when they are flexible and are prepared to employ more than one strategy.

For those who prefer a more simplified approach, Schlossberg's model can be reframed in the form of these four questions for your client to ponder:

- What is happening now? (Situation)
- How am I doing? (Self)
- What do I need? (Support)
- How do I cope? (Strategies)

Cognitive Information Processing (CIP)

Cognitive Information Processing is a set of theoretical perspectives dealing with how we sequence and execute cognitive events. It focuses on what happens between input (receiving information) and output (executing the information). Framed like a pyramid, CIP theory purports that all career problem-solving and decision-making involve self-knowledge, occupational knowledge, decision-making skills and metacognitions.

CIP Theory

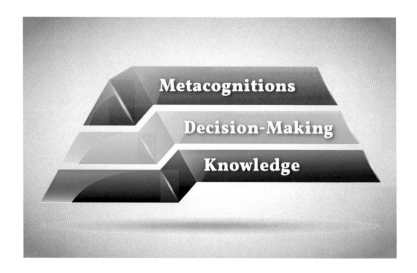

Level 1: Knowledge Domain
(knowing about myself, knowing about my options)

Self-knowledge: At the base of the pyramid, this step includes information about a client's employment interests, skills, values, aptitudes and personality attributes. These can be obtained from card sorts, inventories, worksheets or online resources like the Self-Directed Search®(SDS).

Occupational Knowledge: Accompanying self-knowledge is occupational information: Researching employers, person-to-person or online networking, employment websites, military-to-civilian skills translators, informational interviews, career and employment fairs.

Level 2: Decision-Making Skills Domain
(knowing how I make decisions)

Using CASVE, a 5-phase decision-making model (communication, analysis, synthesis, valuing, and execution), will help the veteran client determine the best first step and also steps for longer-term goals. In layperson's terms, CASVE can be reframed by asking the following questions:

- Communication – What is the gap?
  What is the issue that needs my attention?
- Analysis – What are the components of the issue(s)?
- Synthesis – What are my alternatives?
- Valuing – Which options are priority?
- Execution – What am I going to do to get to the outcomes I want?

The authors of the CASVE model suggest this sequence for delivering career interventions:[54]

- Step 1 – Conduct initial interview with client.

- Step 2 – Do a preliminary assessment to determine client's readiness.

- Step 3 – Work with client to define the career problem(s) and analyze causes.

- Step 4 – Collaborate with client to formulate achievable problem-solving and decision-making goals.

- Step 5 – Provide clients with a list of activities and resources they need (individual learning plans).

- Step 6 – Require clients to execute their individual learning plans.

- Step 7 – Conduct a summative review of client progress and generalize new learning to other career problems.

Level 3: Metacognitions Domain
(thinking about my decision making)

At this stage clients analyze (executive processing) the decisions they have made. They ask: "How am I feeling about this decision?" By probing for any negative thoughts the client has that might impact the job-search process, career practitioners can challenge the negative thoughts and work with the client to alter negative self-messages. Examples of negative thoughts can be "I'm not good enough," "No one will hire me because of my disability," and so on.

The authors of CIP have also developed the Career Thoughts Inventory (CTI) which helps to measure "dysfunctional thinking" in the career decision-making process such as anxiety about making a career commitment, confusion or external conflicts. Accompanying the CTI is the Career Thoughts Inventory Workbook. It helps clients in reframing the negative thoughts identified. This is also where developing individualized learning plans can ensure clients have tangible tools and strategies to keep them on track moving forward.

Mary Buzzetta and Shirley Rowe believe that Cognitive Information Processing can also be used to help transitioning military personnel who are facing real or imagined career or employment barriers.[55] For example, moving from a highly structured and team-oriented work environment to a civilian workplace that is less structured and individual-oriented can be construed as a barrier, generating negative self-talk like "I'll never learn to function in a place where the rules are always changing." There is also the loss of identity the released member experiences—loss of role and status.

By exploring the client's career thoughts and applying the CASVE model, career practitioners can provide a safe place for clients to air their feelings, help them reframe and eventually move on to resolution.

Solution-focused Coaching

"What if a miracle happened and whatever problem you're experiencing right now got fixed—what would your life look like?"

This is called the "miracle" question and is asked by some coaches using the solution-focused approach.[56] No longer restricted to the realm of counselling, solution-focused coaching operates on two key premises: (1) individualized and personalized coaching solutions work best, and (2) people each have the ability to solve their own problem. It is respectful, collaborative and brief. Here are the steps for your client:

1. Acknowledge the problem.
   How is this a problem? How does it affect me?

2. Define the difference you want to achieve.
   How would my future look if this were not a problem?

3. Identify what will help you achieve the outcome you desire.

4. Focus on doing more of what works and less of what doesn't.

The veteran who cannot find work and is mired in negativity or hopelessness, the client who has little patience for a drawn out process-oriented counselling strategy, or the individual who is having difficulty articulating how her military career has equipped her with skills employers want—all can benefit from a solution-focused coaching approach.

Strength-based Coaching/Counselling

Often clients solicit the assistance of career professionals to help them find a particular job without first determining if the job is a good fit. Helping the client assess the strengths they possess and learn how to articulate these to a prospective employer can be very liberating. Strengths can come in the form of personality attributes, competencies, aptitudes or skills. Ask:

- When are you at your best?
- Describe a peak moment in your life.
- What gives you energy and makes you feel good about yourself?
- Tell me about three good things in your life?

The above questions are meant to draw out a person's inherent and energizing capacities. Energizing is the operative word in this approach. Infused with elements of positive psychology, strength-based coaching focuses not on the things clients do poorly, but on helping them become better at the things they do well.

Watch what happens when you ask a client to talk about a peak moment or engagement in an activity that uses their best skills. Her face lights up. His eyes shine. She sounds articulate and confident. He sounds excited.

Now see the difference when you ask that same person to talk about their weaknesses. The posture droops. The energy drops. The sun sets.

As with the solution-focused approach, strength-based coaching/counselling can be an excellent model to use with veterans looking for work.

Legacy Careers® Approach

As noted in Chapter 2, retirement from military service can occur at the normal retirement age or at a relatively young age. Whether younger or older, the veteran who has amassed skills, experiences, relationships and knowledge and wants to focus future efforts on addressing issues, problems, challenges and opportunities that matter to them can benefit from the Legacy Careers® Approach. It involves:

- Taking stock
- Identifying meaning
- Creating a plan
- Leaving a legacy

This approach does not focus on translating military experience to fit a civilian job posting. Rather, it is concerned with providing tools and approaches to help the veteran establish an identity in civilian life that is meaningful and forward-looking. The Legacy Careers® Approach acknowledges that there is a broad spectrum of possibilities between continuing to do the same work and doing nothing. It begs the question: "What do I want to use the next phase of my life to do?"

For the career practitioner, rather than starting with the Knowledge Domain outlined in level 1 of the CIP approach (self-assessment and career options), we can help focus the client on the essential criteria that must be satisfied so that they will feel secure and satisfied in their next career.

- What do I need and want?
- What do I care about?
- What are my innate talents (as opposed to learned skills)?

- What impact should my work have? What problems do I want to be part of solving?

The Legacy Careers® Approach does not assume that people will continue on a linear career path, remain in the same industry or maintain the same level or rank as in their mid-careers. Instead, it allows them to take a step back from titles, roles and specific job duties to identify what meaning they want their work to have and what steps they will need to take to move from where they are now to where they want to be. Often, the process involves retraining, internships, temporary jobs or a multi-step plan.

The Legacy approach identifies what clients will be doing over the next 6 months, 1–2 years and 5–10 years to continually grow and evolve into their full "legacy career." By taking a 10- to 20-year horizon, practitioners can work with transitioning military clients to build a plan that

- meets their short-term and long-term needs,
- focuses on their innate talents (as opposed to areas where they have acquired skills),
- involves work that they care about, and
- makes an impact that is recognized in today's market.

The above approaches/methodologies are by no means the only options. Career practitioner Melissa Martin recommends hope-centered coaching, resilience coaching and mindfulness training.[57] You might prefer to use your own trusted and proven techniques.

Support Networks for At-risk Veterans

For those whose careers have been interrupted due to injury or illness, the choice to leave military service may not have been voluntary. Coming from a culture where employability is tied to deployability and deployability is a requirement for remaining in the service—where "fitness" is strength—asking for help could prove difficult for ill or injured veterans. Not only that, very few civilians have an appreciation for the rigors of combat. Most do not want to hear or talk about it. In many instances, career coaches caution veterans about sharing the details of combat duties in resumés or at job interviews.

We already established in Chapter 1 that connecting to peer networks is a key component in helping veterans adapt to life after military service. Let's take a look at some of the services available to help vets cope with illnesses acquired during service:

Operational Stress Injury and Social Support (OSISS) [www.osiss.ca]

In the waiting area of a clinic in 2001, a couple of injured CAF personnel struck up a conversation. That serendipitous encounter served as the genesis for OSSIS. Operational Stress Injury and Social Support (OSISS), a partnership between CAF and Veterans Affairs, provides peer-to-peer support to CAF members, veterans or families of former CAF members dealing with the impact of operational stress injuries (OSIs). An OSI is defined as any persistent psychological difficulty that is a result of operational duties while in military service. OSIs include post-traumatic stress disorders (PTSDs), anxiety, depression or any condition that impacts one's ability to function in daily tasks. Since its inception, OSISS has created a nationwide Peer Support Network in more than 20 locations offering CAF members, veterans and their families peer-to-peer support, a listening ear and referrals as needed.

Wounded Warriors
[www.woundedwarriors.ca]

Wounded Warriors acts as an umbrella organization providing programs and funds for a spectrum of peer-focused care for CAF veterans. Relying heavily on the healing powers of nature and animals, Wounded Warriors programs include PTSD Service Dogs, PTSD Equine, fly fishing, wilderness tours and a reflection park. It also helps fund the Veterans Transition Network and the Veterans Emergency Transition Services.

Veterans Transition Network
[www.vtncanada.org]

Offers transition courses to CAF members and families. Co-facilitated by CAF vets and psychologists/counsellors, the free courses cover a range of transition issues including reconnecting with family, PTSD, career and other resources. Each course runs for 10 days (three weekends).

Veterans Emergency Transition Services (VETS) Canada
[www.vetscanada.org]

Helps homeless and at-risk vets reintegrate into civilian life. VETS was launched in 2010–11 when CAF veteran Jim Lowther came to the realization that many fellow veterans had not made successful transitions to civilian life. Some had lost their families, were suicidal, homeless, unemployed or struggling to cope with mental or physical illnesses. VETS helps veterans move from the street or shelters to affordable housing, access health care and benefits/services, and find suitable employment. VETS is now a nationwide movement, a registered non-profit charity with a network of over 135,000 and hundreds of volunteers, and a VAC-approved service provider.

See Chapter 8 for a fuller listing of support services in different areas. Remember that different vets have different needs! Remember too to collaborate with other career practitioners to share and gain knowledge.

KEY LEARNING

* Readiness is key to career planning and decision-making.

* Transition assessment can help clients who are "stuck."

* Negative thoughts can interfere with career plans.

* Career transition planning might include taking a long view (legacy).

* Support networks can help with coping and adaptation.

* * *

*The most recent edition of
[Richard N. Bolles']*
What Color Is Your Parachute?
*has a special veterans section entitled
"A 10-minute crash course
for returning veterans."*

*The only person who is educated
is the one who has learned
how to learn and change.*

—Carl Rogers, psychologist[58]

"An incredible experience!"

Sasha joined the CAF Reserves in 1999 and five years later decided to enter the Regular Forces where she is still serving.

While in university she had been fortunate to secure a co-op placement with the Department of National Defence, working in public relations. During that placement and at the young age of 21 she had a turning-point moment. "It was the first time someone trusted me with a big project."

Sasha's big media project turned out to be a huge success, making front-page news. Excitement about the success of her efforts, however, was not sufficient to make her join the CAF. "I never believed I had what it took to be in the military so I went back to university and completed my degree."

After graduating from university and working in a number of contract positions Sasha was ready for something with a bit more permanence.

"In 1999, I was walking to meet a client and ran into the same officer who I had worked with earlier. I told him that I really enjoyed working for him and I would do this again. He then told me about the Reserve and he helped me through the recruiting process.

"I joined because I really liked the person I was going to work with. He was a very inspiring leader with no prejudice."

According to Sasha, her military career has provided her with "lots of opportunities to travel and to test my limits. I became a leader and learned how to manage people and projects. It has been an incredible experience."

So why is Sasha thinking of leaving?

"It is time to use this experience to do other things."

Now a Major, Sasha thinks she will miss the structure of military life. "There is comfort in it, knowing that you are taken care of by your supervisor (leader), evaluated, reviewed, supported, and mentored."

At this point she is exploring career options outside the CAF, networking with friends and previous colleagues.

"I have a great network of friends who know me and what I can accomplish. They have been very helpful."

CHAPTER 6 –

The Education/
Qualification Conundrum

Recommendation 3 of a 2014 report by the Senate's Subcommittee on Veterans Affairs calls on the Canadian Armed Forces and the Department of National Defence to make the VAC transition interview mandatory for all personnel who are to be released.[59]

In 2011, President Obama signed the Veterans Opportunity to Work (VOW) Act. This mandated that all US veterans participate in pre-separation counselling prior to leaving military service. The counselling covers three aspects: benefits, occupations and a gap analysis.

Why do Canada and US see the need to mandate something like this? The answer is to ensure military members have discussed their post-release needs and are made aware of the benefits and services available should they need assistance.

As Marc's story (see **page 105**) so poignantly illustrates, preparation is everything; he did not do the preplanning and it would have made all the difference. Accessing the CAF's Career Transition Services far in advance of leaving military service will prompt members to give some thought to life after the military. To consider questions like "What do I want to do?" and "What will I need to do it?"

Asking "What will I need to do it?" allows service members to examine their current education or experiences and the need for further education or training. It might also include exploring the requirements institutions look for so that advance preparation can be done. Be that as it may, we do not always do what we need to do when we should do it, so let's deal with the now.

Getting Credit for Military Training and Education

In Chapter 2 we saw a list of the many CAF training centres and educational institutions. Here's the problem: Much military training and education is military specific.

This has implications not just for civilian employability but also for receiving civilian educational recognition. Even though each CAF member is encouraged to create an individualized learning plan, if that plan did not take post-military life into consideration, it could be limiting.

Civilian institutions have a different credentialing standard. There is also on the whole a lack of understanding on the part of civilians about military education and training. Getting recognition from civilian institutions and employers for time and training received in the military is therefore not easy.

Where then does that leave, for example, our newly transitioned artillery soldier who might be considering a career as a computer operator (see Introduction, **page 18**)? Better yet, let's say she is successful in getting hired by a company to work in said occupation. Will her lack of civilian educational credentials impede upward mobility within that company? What if, after a few years with the company, she decides to seek employment elsewhere. Will the educational "shortfall" rear its head again? These questions hint at some of the educational challenges an unprepared veteran might encounter.

While almost all Canadian universities and community colleges offer Prior Learning Assessment and Recognition (PLAR),[60] this service is not very well advertised to the military members who need it, or else what it offers does not shave much time off the requirements to secure a diploma or degree.

There is currently no uniform Canadian guide to help institutions determine civilian equivalencies to military experience and training. This is a huge area of need in Canada. All is not lost however. In recognition of the plight of veterans, and through a number of advocacy initiatives, there are educational institutions that actively promote and provide credit for military service. Below is a list of some of these institutions.

Educational Institutions Providing Credit and Training

Algonquin College [www.algonquincollege.com/military] provides credit recognition for the following military occupations:

- CAF Management Support Clerk

- CAF Basic Military Qualification
  (New Defence and Security Certificate Program)

- CAF Geomatics Technician

- CAF Military Police

The **Military Support Office** at the **University of Manitoba** [http://umanitoba.ca/faculties/coned/military], in partnership with DND, recognizes and facilitates the education and training of military personnel in various ways:

- Provides degree credit for certain
  military courses and training

- Oversees a reduced residency requirement
  for selected degree programs

- Authorizes withdrawals and/or tuition reimbursement
  if/when military duty conflicts with courses

- Provides academic advising and degree program planning

Military members can enter their Military Occupation Code (MOC) and their level of training into the university's Military Credit Transfer Database [http://umanitoba.ca/extended/military/credit] to determine (unofficially) if they are eligible for credits. They can submit their Member Personnel Record Resume (MPRR) and transcripts from other post-secondary institutions to receive an official assessment of transfer credits, at no cost.

Athabasca University [www.athabascau.ca] will accept transfer credits for military experience so that a student can reduce the number of courses required to receive an Athabasca degree. Military members must first apply and be accepted to Athabasca and must have their military experience evaluated by the Military Support Office at the University of Manitoba.

The **Legion Military Skills Conversion Program** at the **British Columbia Institute of Technology** (BCIT) [www.bcit.ca/legion] is open to both former and current members of the CAF Regular and Reserve Forces plus the National Guard. It allows them to fast-track their education by earning BCIT credits in degree/diploma programs such as HR, Operations Management, Business Operations, GIS, Construction, and Business Information Technology.

The **Canadian Forces Program** at **Northern Alberta Institute of Technology** (NAIT) [www.nait.ca/canadian-forces-program.htm] allows CAF personnel access to a variety of courses, upgrading options and full-time programs. NAIT grants advance credits to CAF members trained in over 13 distinct occupational areas, including Aerospace Telecommunications, Cook, Marine Engineer, Resource Management Clerk, Weapons Technician, and Military Leadership.

University of New Brunswick (UNB) [www.unb.ca/cel/ military/credit.html] will assess military training for possible credit to any of its programs. Applicants need to provide their MPRR, course reports for language training, relevant transcripts and course descriptions, a completed UNB application for admission and pay a fee.

Fanshawe College is part of a **consortium of schools** that has joined with Canada Company to establish educational pathways whereby those with military training and experience can obtain prior-learning credit based on both the schools' and provincial guidelines. Other members of the consortium include BCIT, NAIT, the Marine Institute of Memorial University and triOS College.

Other institutions and organizations offering educational opportunities include FDM Group, The Institute for Performance and Learning (formerly the Canadian Society for Training and Development), Maritime Drilling Schools, QQC Recruiting Limited, and Industrial Marine Training and Applied Research Centre (IMTARC).

Business and Entrepreneurship Programs

The **New Business Start-up Program** at Centennial College [www.centennialcollege.ca/coe] is useful for CAF veterans interested in starting their own business. Offered by the Centre for Entrepreneurship, and boasting a 95% business success rate, the online New Business Start-up Program teaches participants how to develop, refine and implement a business plan. Interested CAF members can consult their Personnel Selection Officer for more information.

Seven-day **Based in Business** boot camps run by **Prince's Operation Entrepreneur** on university campuses across Canada teach transitioning military members the basics of entrepreneurship. In 2016 boot camps, are scheduled for Université Laval, Dalhousie University, Queen's University, Memorial University, and the University of Regina.

Legion Lions' Lair and **Mindworks** at the **British Columbia Institute of Technology** (BCIT) [www.bcit.ca/legion/entrepreneurship.shtml] are also available for veterans who want to explore entrepreneurship.

Trade Certification

Former CAF military personnel with experience in skilled trades such as plumber, cook, automotive service technician, electrician, carpentry, welder, refrigeration, heavy-duty equipment operator, and more can apply to write provincial or territorial exams to receive Red Seal certification [http://www.red-seal.ca/contact/pt-eng.html]. Two examples:

- **Ontario College of Trades**
  [www.collegeoftrades.ca/veterans]

- **Saskatchewan Apprenticeship and Trade Certification Commission**
  [http://saskapprenticeship.ca/workers/experienced-workers/former-canadian-military-personnel/]

Employment Equivalencies
for Military Experience

We have already established that many civilian employers and educational administrators do not understand military training and education or know how to determine civilian job equivalents. Below are a few tools that can help to address this gap:

Military to Civilian Trades

In Appendix 1 you will find the Military to Civilian Trades table. Developed in-house by the CAF Career Transition Services, this 8-page document provides civilian equivalents to over 350 military jobs.

Military Occupations and Related Civilian Occupations (MOC to NOC) [www.forces.gc.ca/en/business-reservist-support/tools-occupations.page]

Another table, Military Occupations and Related Civilian Occupations, provides National Occupational Classification (NOC) equivalents to Military Occupation Codes (MOCs). Unfortunately, the database is limited in the number of occupations that are showcased. And for most of the operational occupations, like those of Artillery Soldier, Infantry Soldier and Armoured Soldier, no equivalent NOC code is provided. It is noted on the site however that combat arms jobs are unique to the military and do not have civilian equivalents. Employers and career practitioners are encouraged to focus on the many transferable skills of the transitioning members who did such jobs (time management, leadership and organizational skills, etc.)

Government of Canada Job Bank
[www.jobbank.gc.ca]

This national database offers job listings, career exploration tools, and job market news. The career exploration component provides information on occupational outlook, wages, and a skills and knowledge checklist which is particularly useful when working with former military members. With the skills and knowledge checklist, job seekers can identify their skills from 10 categories and their knowledge from nine areas. Results yield a Skills and Knowledge Profile showing related occupations, skills matches and knowledge needed. By clicking on the occupations, one can view all the current jobs available by region.

Another resource that has some limited usefulness is **O*NET** [www.onetonline.org]. O*NET is the primary source for occupational information in the United States. Like the Canadian Job Bank, it includes a database of occupations and career exploration and assessment tools for those finding or changing careers. **My Next Move for Veterans** [www.mynextmove.org/vets] is a sub-component of O*NET. In the "Find careers like your military job" section one can enter the name of a military occupation, click "Find," and be presented with a list of civilian equivalents from closest to farthest match. Bear in mind that the nature and content of CAF military occupations might differ from those of the US, so this resource has limited usefulness.

Further Development Needed

As you can see, more work is needed on the Canadian academic front to create a nationally recognized credentialing process for CAF members. Models from the US can be examined and adapted to do this. In addition, further development of the Military to Civilian Trades document and its inclusion as a component of the Job Bank database (similar to My Next Move) would go a long way in helping CAF members more readily determine some of the career options open to them after release from military service.

This concludes the section on pre-employment readiness. What comes next is an examination of the needs of military spouses, the impact of the military lifestyle on their career development and suggestions for career building.

KEY LEARNING

* Several educational institutions across the country offer credit for military experience.

* Provincial and territorial certification is available for those in the skilled trades.

* The Military Occupations and Related Civilian Occupations table provides National Occupational Classification (NOC) equivalents for military jobs. Another tool for identifying civilian equivalents to military jobs is the Military to Civilian Trades table (Appendix 1), which could be further developed.

* In the United States, My Next Move for Veterans (O*NET) generates civilian job equivalents.

* More Canadian "credentialing" resources for military experience/skills are needed.

YVONNE'S FAVOURITES

The **Military to Civilian Trades** *table in Appendix 1 lists over 350 civilian jobs and their military equivalents.*

The **Military Transfer Credit Database** *at the University of Manitoba allows CAF personnel to enter their Military Occupation Code (MOC) and their level of training to determine if they are eligible for credits.*

PART IV:
STRENGTH BEHIND
THE UNIFORM

Photo credit: Military Family Services

Successfully supporting families must be understood as the critical, 'no-fail' requirement that it is for the Canadian Forces.

—Pierre Daigle, CAF Ombudsman[61]

"Be resourceful, resilient and persistent"

Kathleen is the spouse of a retired member of the Canadian Armed Forces. Her husband medically released after 22 years of service only two years ago. Hers is a typical story of a military spouse making the best of whatever challenges the CAF tossed her way.

"When I was young, I remember my dad encouraging me to join the CAF. I had no intention. I was going to get my Ph.D. in life sciences and live an academic life," said Kathleen.

Life had other plans for her. She met her future husband, Bob, while she was still a junior in university. He was already a member of the CAF. What did young Kathleen know about the military? "I had no perception. To be honest, I was so green. No one in my family, that I was aware of, had served. One of my best friend's brothers was in the military. All I learned, I learned from her. Good job, good pension, good prospects and travel. So, basically I knew I would probably live on base and definitely travel."

She had a choice to make when she and Bob graduated from university: let him go for good and go live the life she had dreamed of, or join him. She chose the latter. "I knew military life would be different than I was used to, but not how dramatically different it was going to be," said Kathleen.

According to her, there was much more to the military lifestyle than she had learned from her friend. There were so many pros and cons. Relocating, making friends and seeing most of Canada were positive, yet challenging, experiences. Living in Private Military Quarters (PMQs) had its benefits and its challenges as well. Not to mention the difficulties of solo parenting while she and Bob were separated by his CAF duties. One major challenge Kathleen never anticipated was in managing her career.

Up to the time of her husband's release, Kathleen had moved seven times. She describes her resumé as "colourful," in a positive way. "You build social capital as part of the military family. Social capital is that social exchange of information and interaction with a variety and number of people you meet, learn from and talk with, to varying degrees. I have met a large number of people in the past 24 years—that is a lot of information transfer and networking."

That social capital has helped her secure job leads and other opportunities. Over the past 24 years Kathleen, the typical military spouse, has worked in telemarketing, golf course beautification, labs, teaching, and sales. She balanced these eclectic jobs with returning to school and raising a child. When her husband was medically released she had to leave her work behind to take care of him for a year, and she continues to balance his care with her day-to-day work life.

"Due to our military lifestyle I've always worked on contract. I tried to address gaps and varied career paths on my resumé. Employers reacted in one of two ways when I disclosed I was a military spouse. Some told me very frankly, 'We can't train you and lose you. You understand?' or they were happy to hear how I managed to balance work, family, and the military lifestyle. Then I had the chance to really sell my resilience, my flexibility and my problem-solving skills," said Kathleen.

The downside of relocating and having to repeatedly give up her employment was not being able to plan or develop her career. Kathleen would have preferred having a strategy to grow and prosper at work, achieve promotions and contribute to a pension. "The job I'm currently doing is the first work I have ever had where I am building my own pension," said Kathleen.

Her career advice to a new military spouse is, "If there is a way to do something you love virtually, or as a mobile business, it is worth pursuing. Use your strengths in being able to relocate, shift jobs, and manage an ever-changing life. Recognize those skills as transferable. Rework and reword your resumé for interviews. Really take time to consider the advantages of being military and speak to those in an interview. Change how employers view that lifestyle."

She would also advise a new spouse that everything related to your career progression takes a bit longer because of relocations, including education, training, and being hired into the right job. "Try to preplan and prepare for any opportunities that might arise."

In looking back on her family's recent transition to civilian life she has a confession to make: "I was scared to death. After doing it for 22 years I was comfortable in the lifestyle." But now, "No one is telling us we have to move anymore. It's exciting to know we can decide where we live now, and I can finally be confident in telling my employer that I am here to stay."

Although her husband has been released, Kathleen's is still a military family and change is ongoing in her life. She is the breadwinner of the family now. Her husband is a veteran learning to cope with permanent injuries and a medical release. Although she is finally able to manage her career, Kathleen has to balance her work with his care.

Thanks to her resilience, flexibility, tenacity and the encouragement of her husband, Kathleen managed to complete a master's degree in Science. She and Bob raised a well-adjusted 17-year old who is on the cusp of joining the CAF.

After 22 years as the spouse of a military member and two years as the spouse of a veteran, she is finally employed full-time and is thriving in her new career.

CHAPTER 7

Career Needs of Military Spouses

Those who serve in occupations to defend and protect our personal and civil liberties strongly benefit from the support of family, mentors, peer networks and service providers. What though do we know of the family members, particularly the civilian or non-serving spouses who serve at home while their loved one is serving their country?

Realities of Life for the Military Family

In November 2013, CAF Ombudsman Pierre Daigle tendered a special report to the Minister of National Defence.[62] This report examined how well the families of today's Canadian Armed Forces were doing. As a preamble to the findings of the report, Daigle provided some important contextual points:

- Canada has been engaged in continuous military operations since 1990.

- This engagement is more complex and challenging than in recent previous military operations.

- The duration and challenges of this type of military engagement have taken a toll on families.

- There has been an increase in the number of family-related complaints to the Department of National Defence and the Canadian Armed Forces.

Daigle's research focused on the families of 370 current and recently retired CAF members. Overall findings indicated that families (1) were proud of their contributions to making their family situations work in spite of the challenges of having a parent or partner in active military duty; and (2) value some of the benefits of military family life, such as more bilingual educational opportunities for their children and the ability to live in different locations. The research also revealed, however, that relocation and deployments cause major disruption and strain on families.

Three realities are constants in the lives of military families:

1. **Mobility**: relocation on average every three to five years within Canada or abroad and over which they have little or no input/influence

2. **Separation**: ongoing or periodic separation associated with deployments and training

3. **Risk**: living with the inherent dangers associated with military training and service

One could argue that these realities are not unique to military families. It's true—they aren't. But while many other professions include one or more of these challenges, very few demand all three. With regards to separation and risk, while the serving partner is working long hours, deployed or on training, the military spouse is the one responsible for keeping the family unit afloat and functioning smoothly. On average, military families relocate three times more often than the average Canadian family, which can contribute to further strain on the spouse. All three realities combined often contribute to a less-than-conventional career path for the military spouse.

The rest of this chapter will focus on military spouses/partners: how their career development and employment prospects are impacted by the military lifestyle, and how career practitioners can help them mitigate some of their common employment challenges.

The Military Spouse: Characteristics and Statistics

The profile of a military spouse includes some or all of these characteristics:

- Military spouses are a talented group of individuals. Due to the nature of the military lifestyle, spouses develop qualities and skills highly valued by employees: problem solving, flexibility, adaptability, critical thinking, organization, resiliency, project management, creativity and leadership.

- Military spouses frequently experience challenges in finding employment and building their careers, resulting in unemployment or underemployment.

- Frequent relocations can limit continuing education opportunities and make it difficult for a spouse to accrue seniority at work.

- When opportunity is scarce, especially in remote military communities, military spouses often settle for jobs that are below their skill level and education, thus limiting their own professional growth and development.

- Military spouses demonstrate incredible resourcefulness by seeking continuing education and/or volunteer experiences when employment opportunities are not available.

- On average, military spouses earn 20% less than their civilian counterparts.[63]

- With the serving partner away due to deployment or training, the spouse has to take on additional responsibilities on the home front that can negatively impact their own career development.

- Many spouses do not recognize the value of their skills and/or how to communicate what they have to offer to employers

- Military spouses are courageous and driven to exceed expectations. They are known to have a "can do" attitude.

There are 61,500 military spouses located across Canada.

- 73% of military spouses are between 25 and 44 years of age[64]
- 13% are male
- 77% report English as first language
- 23% list French as first language
- 62% have a post-secondary diploma/degree[65]
- 82% live in civilian communities[66]
- 64% are spouses of Regular Force members; 36% are spouses of Reservists

We also know a few things about the nature of CAF spousal employment:[67]

- 6.1% are self-employed
- 8.2% are managers
- 9.4% work in retail
- 24.1% work in administrative/clerical roles
- 31.1% are professionals
- 21.1% work in other fields

What these statistics tell us is that CAF military spouses are educated, hard-working, adaptable, mobile, diverse, and in the prime of life.

Employment Challenges for the Military Spouse

Let's recap the employment challenges military spouses face: Military spouses as a group face a number of employment challenges: difficulty in developing their careers or finding and sustaining employment; being overlooked for promotions due to inconsistent or short-term employment history; inability to accrue seniority due to frequent relocations; having their career development or professional training impeded based on location; facing limited employment prospects when posted in small or rural communities. Such challenges not only affect spouses' career development, they also impact the financial stability of their families.

The second phase of a project undertaken by the Director General Military Personnel Research and Analysis examined the employment status and income of female military spouses in comparison to the spouses of police, federal public servants and other civilians.[68] Key findings of this project include the following:

- Female partners of CAF members were less likely to be employed compared to female spouses of police, federal public servants, and other civilians.

- Female spouses of Officers were less likely to be employed compared to female spouses of non-commissioned members (NCMs).

- CAF spouses/partners earned less money than the spouses/partners of civilians, police, and public servants.

- Female spouses of NCMs earned less on average than female spouses of Officers.

The final report for the project further explained that for CAF spouses/partners, the top motivating factor for working was "to pay bills, cover expenses."

A CBC article citing a Statistics Canada report on family changes since 1976 notes that "few Canadian families can afford to live on one income as many did in 1976."[69] In addition, the report found that 75 percent of families with two income earners were both working full-time in 2014 in comparison to 66 percent back in 1976. This tells us that in order for most two-parent families to be financially comfortable, both parents work outside the home.

How then do we help the military spouse whose opportunity to earn a living is severely impacted by the military lifestyle?

Overcoming Employment Challenges

Spouses can take creative steps to limit the need to restart their career every time they move. Career practitioners can encourage spouses to think outside the box and strategically explore careers that have the possibility to sustain them through military life and afterwards. Pamela McBride and Lori Cleymans offer some useful suggestions[70]:

1. **Create a Career Lattice:** A lattice aptly symbolizes a career path that recognizes value in the variety of experiences one has (volunteer, education, training, employment, entrepreneurship, etc.). Taken as a whole, how do these experiences demonstrate one's value to an employer? This is where career practitioners can help military spouses in assessing their composite of experiences and creating a career path that strategically moves them towards work that is more satisfying.

2. **Increase marketability with each move:** Each new move, each new job/volunteer position, each new training or educational venture provides skill-building opportunities. Practitioners can facilitate the fleshing out of this information by asking questions— What tasks were you responsible for accomplishing? What things were you the go-to person for?—and helping spouses use the answers to create strong accomplishment statements. Career practitioners can also help spouses set short- and long-term career goals by encouraging the documentation of skills acquired through various experiences, so that each new move can be viewed through the lens of strategic skill-building.

3. **Understand the range of professional development opportunities:** It is tiring to have to look for work over and over again. Sometimes there is no work to be found. Instead of giving up, military spouses can explore ways to continue growing their careers through education and training. Practitioners knowledgeable about the careers or skills that are in demand can help

clients make informed decisions regarding continuing education opportunities which have the best probability of leading to a sustainable and portable career.

4. **Learn the language of the job market:** "Research" is probably one of the most hated words in career planning. It is especially difficult to do for the spouse whose hands are already full juggling life and family responsibilities. Frustrating or not, research is necessary. Career practitioners can work with spouses to prioritize the research tasks and focus on doing one thing at a time.

5. **Create a career portfolio and document accomplishments:** Developing and maintaining a career portfolio to keep resumés, letters of recommendation, transcripts, certificates/licences, awards, memberships, job descriptions, volunteer experiences, and even performance evaluations will help military spouses easily access information when they need it. In addition, creating a list of transferable skills along with supporting statements will help the spouse articulate to employers how these skills match the employer's needs.

6. **Use social media to build networks:** A professional social media presence is recommended for all serious job seekers. For example, a LinkedIn profile can showcase qualifications, testimonials, areas of expertise, professional memberships and accomplishments. Furthermore, professional social media sites provide rich opportunities to grow one's network and reach out for advice if and when needed. There are job search groups for military spouses on both LinkedIn and Facebook.

7. **Access military spousal network:** Military spouses maintain strong loyalties to each other and often share and post information about job opportunities.

The sayings "turn lemons into lemonade" or "if you can't change your circumstances, change your perspective" are fitting in this discussion of overcoming challenges.

What if the military spouse gives some thought to exploring "portable" or flexible careers? How about telecommuting? Running a home-based business? These are great ideas that we will examine below, but let's face it: some careers are just not portable.

Even for careers that on the surface seem to be portable options (nursing, teaching, pharmacy, medicine, social work, etc.) credential transfers can be problematic when licensures are provincially or territorially managed. That said, the intergovernmental Agreement on Internal Trade (AIT) ensures that workers certified for a regulated occupation in one province or territory can, upon application, be certified for that occupation anywhere in Canada without any additional training, experience or assessment. But here is the caveat: Under the current framework, provinces can post exceptions to particular trades or occupational groups, thereby overriding the spirit of the AIT. Case in point: To date, 12 provinces and territories have posted a total of 43 exceptions affecting a number of occupational groups (dental hygienists, denturists, drinking water system operators, lawyers, licensed practical nurses, medical radiation technologists, midwives, nurse practitioners, paramedics, podiatrists, psychologist, safety code officers, social workers, water well drillers).

This is a good example of how problematic and frustrating licensure can be for a military spouse/partner who may be employed in one of the identified groups and who may be required to move across provinces every two to three years.[71]

Other careers, like sales, may offer career flexibility but can sometimes be accompanied by financial unpredictability.

The truth of the matter is, sometimes the jobs our clients desire are just not available. When this happens, and after they've come to terms with the reality, we can often nudge them in a new direction.

- Work differently. See work differently. Does it always have to be done in its traditional setting?

- Help clients to leverage technology and social media to create opportunities. If your client used to teach or counsel and there are no local jobs, could he do e-teaching, e-tutoring, or e-counselling?

- Encourage clients to ask for what they need. One spouse, on receiving the news that her family was about to be posted elsewhere, did just that. She presented a case to her employer that demonstrated how she could continue to do the same job working from home. She anticipated and addressed all the employer's concerns as well as how her solution would save the employer money. Even though the company had never done this previously, her request was granted. She even received a promotion while working from home.

A change of perspective is sometimes all that is required to get our clients moving in a new direction.

✳ ✳ ✳

*For the extroverted military spouse,
working in direct sales—from knives to
cosmetics, candles to insurance—provides
great opportunities to connect with people
in each new community.*

Thinking Outside the Box:
Portable Career Options

Back to the idea of portable careers. We can help spouses who are tired of the hassle of having to worry about getting a job every time they relocate by encouraging them to explore what I have dubbed "beyond borders" careers. Here are some popular examples of such careers:

- Consultant
- Virtual office assistant: data entry, office administration/support, bookkeeping, research, word processing
- Direct sales
- Online tutor or teacher
- Home-based child-care provider (or summer day camps or after-school care)
- Writer/editor/translator
- Graphic designer
- Fitness trainer/yoga instructor
- Pet care – dog walker, pet sitter
- Home-based catering service provider
- Telephone fundraiser
- Mystery shopper
- Paid survey-taker
- Blogger
- Call center representative

Career practitioners and job seekers can explore more work-from-home opportunities by reviewing CERIC's Legitimate Work-From-Home Opportunities project, found online at http://ceric.ca/project/legitimate-opportunities-to-work-from-home/. Also, most major employment search engines like Indeed or Monster includes home-based career options. Applying due diligence, one can weed out the scams, find legitimate opportunities, and take control of one's career destiny.

Addressing Employer Biases in the Interview

We have already documented the many skills that military spouses posses as a direct result of living the military lifestyle: adaptability, flexibility, problem solving, creativity and so on. What the research also tells us is that many do not recognize these skills or know how to communicate them to a prospective employer. For the military spouse wishing to pursue traditional employment, the key to success is preparation.

For example, how do we equip spouses to address "problems" employers might be thinking but not asking about? Here are four questions employers might be asking themselves about your client:

1. Why have you had so many employment changes and/ or jobs not related to your education or training?

2. Why do you have so many volunteer or continuing education experiences?

3. Why is your resumé in a functional, not chronological, format?

4. Why should I bother hiring you? You'll be gone in a few months.

Using some of the elements of hope-centered coaching, we can help military spouses plan responses to address the biases in such questions. Let's work through possible responses for a fictional client, Mary Jane Smith. You'll find her resumé on **pages 164-165**. Notice that Mary Jane has a gap in her professional experience as well as continuing education and volunteer experiences. Notice too that she has held varied positions for short periods of time (1–2 years). Mary Jane exemplifies how the military lifestyle could impact a military spouse's employment history.

Employer bias #1: In reviewing the resume of a military spouse who has held many short-term jobs, jobs unrelated to education or training, or jobs entry-level in nature, an employer might assume that the candidate is unambitious, lazy, an underperformer or unreliable.

Addressing employer bias #1: Through practice interviews, career practitioners can help clients learn to communicate the reason for the seeming deficits while keeping the focus on the fact that, despite the challenges, they were able to acquire skills. A possible answer for someone like Mary Jane might be: "Every move means searching for a new job. It means conducting market research to see what opportunities are available in my new community, networking, stepping out of my comfort zone, and doing what needs to be done to advance both my own career development and meet our financial needs. Sometimes the work that is available is different from what I was trained to do, offers lower compensation or is contractual in nature. In every one of these jobs, I ensured I was a major contributor to the organization and not a drag on resources. My previous employers will all attest to my reliability, responsibility and strong work ethic."

Employer bias #2: A resumé that shows a higher-than-normal amount of volunteer or continuing education experience may cause an employer to wonder if the spouse is seriously interested in working.

Addressing employer bias #2: A possible answer could be: "In many of the locations where my spouse was posted there were no jobs to be found. Because I have created a strategic plan for building my career, I determined that in situations where I could not find paid employment I would instead seek out specific volunteer or educational opportunities that would help me develop skills in line with my strategic plan. I believe in being resourceful and maximizing the opportunities at my disposal rather than bemoaning things I cannot change." What employer would not be impressed!

Employer bias #3: A candidate who has submitted a functional rather than a chronological resumé must be hiding something.

Addressing employer bias #3: A possible answer could be: "I have chosen a non-chronological resumé format to showcase my experiences. Every work opportunity I have had has taught me something different. The tasks may have been the same, but the way I have had to work or the people I have worked with meant that I needed to consistently modify my approach or methods to get the job done. I wanted to communicate the broad range of skills I have that can help an organization meet its goals. Longevity in a job does not necessarily mean that a person is being effective. I know how to work hard. I am a creative problem-solver, have had to project-manage all our moves and apply critical-thinking skills to every new posting challenge. These are the qualities I can bring to this job."

Employer bias #4: Military families are always on the move. It does not make sense to hire a military spouse or invest in their training. They will be gone before I can reap the benefits of my investment.

Addressing employer bias #4: The reality is that the normal duration of a military posting is anywhere from 3 to 5 years (this may vary based on circumstances). In 2011, 20 percent of military families surveyed had been in their current location for 3 to 5 years and 30 percent had been in their current location more than 5 years.[72] So even though mobility is a characteristic of military life, the frequency of moves does not affect all military members to the same degree.

Advocating for and with Military Spouses

The sample responses above are meant to illustrate the vital role that military spouses can play in shaping their own career destinies. Career practitioners can teach them how to advocate for themselves and how to look at their experiences through strength-based lenses. Their adaptability, resilience and courage should not be taken for granted by them or anyone else.

Of course, raising employer awareness about the spousal component of the military lifestyle and its impact on career development will help mitigate the biases and misconceptions. Then, to get to the substance of what the candidate brings to the table, the employer can ask behavioural or situational interview questions, focus on the candidate's strengths rather than their history, and suspend judgement about the reason for a candidate's job changes.

Katie Ochin, Employment and Entrepreneurship Program Manager with CAF Military Family Services, sums up the recommendations for career practitioners working with military spouses this way:

1. Military spouses are resilient, adaptable and strong, but they may need assistance demonstrating these strengths in their employment applications. Taking them through a skills inventory exercise may be effective.

2. Encourage military spouses to explore mobile employment and telecommuting opportunities.

3. Encourage military spouses to explore online training and development.

4. Review military spouses' answers to key interview questions and work together to decide how an unorthodox employment history can be addressed in a strength-based way.

5. Teach military spouses how to advocate for themselves and the skills they bring to the job market.

In addition to paying the bills and covering living expenses, military spouses are interested in finding personal fulfillment, maintaining their skills and career status, and gaining independence. They are motivated to work and know how to work hard. They have been doing it for a long time.

***

Military Family Services:
A Network of Support

Military Family Services (MFS) comprises a vast network of resources and services for military families. From toolkits to partnerships, MFS gives CAF family members access to skilled professionals, networking opportunities, employment training and other services designed to support their needs.

In the area of the employability of non-serving military spouses, MFS is working on various initiatives to raise employer awareness and make a case for hiring military spouses. For example, in fall 2015, MFS and Canada Company launched the MET Spouse project (Military Employment Transition Program for Spouses) that was designed after Canada Company's Military Employment Transition (MET) Program for veterans. This program connects participating spouses to a network of national military-spouse–friendly employers who understand the inherent strengths of this workforce and are open to exploring flexible employment opportunities and internal transfers when a spouse is relocated due to a partner's military posting.

Visit the MFS website, www.familyforce.ca, for updated information as well as the locations of Military Family Resource Centres. See Chapter 8, Health and Well-Being, for a sampling of the services offered by MFS and Military Family Resource Centres.

Sample resumé

Mary Jane Smith
123 Main Street, Ottawa, ON K1Z 5Z0
janesmith@gmail.com • (613) 888-1234

SUMMARY OF QUALIFICATIONS

- **Marketing and sales expertise** - Formally trained in marketing and marketing analysis; participated in industry trade shows; designed promotional materials
- **Advanced sales management experience** - 5 years of experience in sales management within the private sector; skilled in strategic sales planning and employee management
- **Strong analytical and problem solving skills** - Able to analyze a situation and address the issue with a calm and professional demeanor
- **Superior leadership and teamwork abilities** - Inherent ability to lead, proven capability to foster a positive work environment, flexible towards the needs of colleagues
- **Resilient and flexible employee** – Developed capacity to continually adapt to changes in a dynamic environment; exceptional work ethic and determination to succeed

EDUCATION

Graduate Diploma in Management   2014–2015
Athabasca University, Distance Education

Bachelor of Commerce   2002–2006
Carleton University, Ottawa, ON
- Graduated with first level honours, majored in Marketing
- Undergraduate Thesis: "Difference in Canadian Consumer Behaviour among Millennials and Generation X"

PROFESSIONAL EXPERIENCE

Account Officer   2012–2014
ABC Press, Fredericton, NB
- Supervised a small group of Account Coordinators and performed team training
- Responded to corporate client account inquiries and performed annual client reviews
- Assisted in the development and implementation of a divisional marketing strategy; participated in industry trade shows and designed new client brochure
- Established a new corporate client referral program that resulted in over $200K of new business within the first year of implementation

Store Manager   2011–2012
Stuff Depot, Suffield, AB
- Recruited, trained and managed a group of 10 employees
- Executed a sales incentive program that increased store sales by 20% within 6 months
- Oversaw inventory management and liaised with product suppliers to ensure timely delivery and superior product quality
- Received "Manager of the Year" in 2011 from Stuff Depot Canada headquarters for increasing overall employee morale and store sale levels

Sample resumé

Sales Representative   2009
CANEX, Suffield, AB
- Operated the cash register and lottery terminal; maintained and balanced daily cash float
- Responded to customer inquiries and managed monthly inventory count
- Prepared in-store displays, stocked shelves and performed housekeeping duties
- Performed daily bank deposits and store opening and closing responsibilities

Marketing and Events Coordinator   2006–2008
Corporate Fun Place, Kingston, ON
- Coordinated corporate event logistics and publicity, including public relations, advertising and collateral material design
- Organized and executed company representation in trade shows, conferences, and seminars
- Led company's annual email marketing initiative, resulting in a 15% increase in customer traffic
- Co-managed an annual marketing budget of $250K; successfully implemented cost savings solutions which resulted in a budget surplus

VOLUNTEER EXPERIENCE

Girl Guide Troop Leader   2009–2011
- Planned and implemented weekly large-group activities and games
- Coordinated 4 adult volunteer crew leaders
- Liaised with parents and guardians regarding upcoming special events
- Reported to Canadian headquarters regarding troop finances and participation numbers

Special Events Coordinator   2008–2010
Military Family Resource Centre, Kingston, ON
- Volunteered 15 hours a week in the office at the centre
- Chaired special events committee; planned and orchestrated two large annual fundraisers which successfully raised over $100K for the centre
- Recruited, motivated and supervised a group of over 30 volunteers

LANGUAGE PROFILE

- Ability to speak, read and write in French and English

TECHNICAL SKILLS

- Proficient in: Microsoft Office Suite, Database Management (Oracle, SAP & Access), Adobe Pro and Photoshop
- General website creation and maintenance knowledge using HTML
- Experienced using social media in corporate settings: Facebook, Twitter, LinkedIn and Instagram

KEY LEARNING

* The life of a military family is disrupted more often than that of most civilian families.

* Military spouses are diverse, educated, hard-working and adaptable.

* Military spouses face unique employment challenges.

* Spouses can consider portable career options.

* Family and other supports are critical to helping military members transition. Military Family Services can help.

PART V:
PROGRAMS AND
RESOURCES

Photo credit: Canadian Forces Combat Camera, DND

When we give cheerfully and accept gratefully, everyone is blessed.

—Maya Angelou, author and poet[73]

"Keep all doors open"

Sergeant McCoy, Infantry, has been a member of the CAF Reserve Force working in a combination of part-time and full-time roles for 10 years and counting.

He joined in high school "out of a desire to learn to defend myself and those I love." Once he discovered that the training entailed using weapons and equipment, McCoy was hooked.

McCoy is still a member of the Reserves. "I have not left fully, just dialled back my commitment significantly compared to what it used to be."

How does working outside the CAF compare with working within? "By far the thing I miss the most is the camaraderie of the Forces. This boils down to the teamwork and friendships that are built during the incredibly stressful and tough times we usually face during training and on deployment and leads to a real feeling of belonging and support by your peers."

McCoy says that although such camaraderie exists in the civilian sector, "the closeness and friendships that were made during my time in the Forces will always be the strongest and longer lasting."

Right now McCoy works as an international sales manager for a Canadian manufacturer of electro-optical equipment. In his current role he is responsible for all of the company's business in Canada, Western Europe, Australia and the Caribbean.

In discussing what helped him as he "dialled" back his military commitment, McCoy says: "Coming from a military background was a huge asset when joining my current employer in that I could relate to the equipment we manufacture. I have real-world experience using a majority of the equipment we produce, giving me an advantage when explaining [its] operation and necessity to our clients and customers. My background has also provided me with several key contacts that have helped me to build my network of agents internationally and to connect to high-ranking military members both inside and outside of Canada."

What were his biggest challenges?

"The biggest adjustments in this career change are that I am now working mostly for myself, with little oversight from our executive team. Although I have the resources to accomplish my job, there is less hand-holding than is experienced in the Canadian Armed Forces, meaning if someone has difficulty they are expected to bring it forward on their own, not wait until a performance review.

Another adjustment for McCoy was this:

"I'm not really managing anyone within the company. Although I manage our international agents, they are not employees of our firm so I have limited control over their actions. This has forced me to find alternative ways to have them comply with our company policies, but has ensured that the job is never dull or too repetitive."

McCoy's advice to someone about to transition to the civilian job market is twofold: take an inventory of your contacts and leverage any connection you can.

"The process of sending out resumés was not successful for me at all. I found that most successful placements are not based on a cold call or blind resumé submission, but instead are due to 'someone who knows someone' that may be looking to hire an ex-military member.

"As more and more employers are realizing the potential that ex-members can bring to their organizations it is important that as many of your contacts know that you are actively looking for employment as well as the direction that you want to go in your job search.

"You never know where the next opportunity may come from, so do your best to keep all doors open for as long as you can."

CHAPTER 8

Services, Programs and Resources

Even though information on programs and resources has been integrated into relevant chapters throughout this guide, here you will find a more detailed list of Canadian military and civilian service providers and areas of specialty. Please bear in mind that this list is neither comprehensive nor exhaustive. Organizations that are doing great work on behalf of CAF members and veterans might have been missed. This is another reason why a forum whereby career professionals can share resources, tools, best practices, learning and knowledge is needed.

Employment

This list comprises organizations that are dedicated to helping transitioning and veteran CAF members prepare for, and secure, employment.

Canada Company [www.canadacompany.ca]

This is a national charity uniting community and corporate leaders to support Canadian troops as they transition from the Canadian Armed Forces. Spearheads the Military Employment Transition (MET) Program, which helps military members, veterans and military spouses transition to careers in the private sector.

Canada Company also hosts a closed LinkedIn group. Canadian Military Employment Transition, for registered MET members and employers: www.linkedin.com/grp/home?gid=8133739

Canadian Armed Forces Transition Services [www.forces.gc.ca/en/caf-community-support-services/caf-transition-services.page]

Provides assistance with second careers, career transition workshops, a vocational program for serving members, referral to sources of employment within the federal public service and to the Military Employment Transition Program provided by Canada Company. Publishes *The Guide to Benefits, Programs, and Services for CAF Members and their Families:* [www.forces.gc.ca/assets/FORCES_Internet/docs/en/caf-community-benefits-ill-injured-deceased/guide-eng.pdf]

Canadian Corps of Commissionaires (CCC) [www.commissionaires.ca]

This is a private, not-for-profit Canadian company employing over 20,000 people in security or protective positions across the country. For businesses, they provide security guard services, security consultation, investigations, and para-policing services. For individuals, they offer fingerprinting services, criminal record checks, record suspensions and pardons and US entry waivers, protection, and more. CCC is one of the largest employers of Canadian vets.

Career Edge Internship Program for Canadian Reservists [www.careeredge.ca/en/job-seekers/cafreservists]

This new program recently announced by the federal government "helps Reservists overcome barriers to employment through paid internships that provide coaching and the knowledge required to successfully transition to the civilian labour force."[74] It is open to young reservists between the ages of 19 and 30 who have at least a high school diploma and have not previously participated in any Career Edge internships. The program began in August 2015, with 50 reservists to be placed in internships in Year 1, 75 in Year 2 and 100 in Year 3, for a total of 225 placements.

Government of Canada Job Bank [www.jobbank.gc.ca]

This national database offers job listings, career exploration tools, and job market news. The career exploration component provides information on occupational outlook, wages, and a skills and knowledge checklist which is particularly useful when working with former military members. With the skills and knowledge checklist, job seekers can identify their skills from 10 categories and their knowledge from nine areas. Results yield a Skills and Knowledge Profile showing related occupations, skills matches and knowledge needed. By clicking on the occupations, one can view all the current jobs available by region.

Helmets to Hardhats (H2H) [www.helmetstohardhats.ca]

Designed to provide opportunities in Canada for anyone who has served, or is currently serving, in the Reserves or Regular Forces. Offers required apprenticeship training to receive journeyperson status for trades in the building and construction industry.

Kijiji Support our Troops Initiative [www.kijiji.ca]

Employers advertising on Kijiji who are interested in hiring veterans have a yellow Veteran Friendly ribbon beside their ads. Select "veteran friendly" from the Featured Ads menu listing to view these employers.

**Military to Civilian Employment
[www.military2civilianemployment.com]**

Offers outgoing members of the CAF bilingual career and interview coaching in person, via Skype, email, and telephone. Also specializes in mental health and the transition from military to civilian employment. Proprietor Melissa Martin also has a members-only LinkedIn group: Military to civilian employment.

**Prince's Operation Entrepreneur
[www.princesoperationentrepreneur.ca]**

Provides servicemen and servicewomen with education, finances and the mentoring needed to launch and maintain successful businesses. Offers Based in Business, seven-day boot camps, on university campuses across Canada.

Prospect Human Services [www.forcesatwork.ca]

Through their Forces@WORK program, Prospect provides "sustainable, supported job placements for releasing CAF members." This program directly connects soldiers with employers and assists them in managing the transition to civilian careers. The Base To Business program helps to inform and educate employers about the skills and attributes candidates with a military background bring to the workplace through seminars and military events.

RBC Ex-military Recruitment Program [www.rbc.com/careers/ex-military.html]

In partnership with Treble Victor (3V), an ex-military networking group founded by two RBC employees, this program develops resources to support the transition of military leaders to careers in business, government and the not-for-profit sector.

Veterans Affairs Canada Career Transition Services (CTS) [www.veterans.gc.ca/eng/services/transition/career]

The Veteran Affairs Canada CTS helps veterans and survivors find civilian employment. Those eligible are reimbursed for these services, up to a lifetime maximum of $1,000. Services include career assessment, aptitude testing, resumé writing, interview skills, one-on-one career counselling, job search assistance, labour market information/analysis, and the services of a professional recruiter.

Health and Well-Being

This list outlines some of the key providers of health and wellness support programs and services for CAF veterans and their families

Canadian Forces Morale and Welfare Services [www.cfmws.com]

Provides overall coordination of CAF morale and welfare programs, service and activities along with support for CAF members and families.

Canadian Service Dog Foundation [www.servicedog.ca]

Helps people suffering with mental illnesses through the use of trained service dogs.

Family Information Line (FIL) [www.familyforce.ca/sites/FIL/EN/]

A bilingual telephone service for the families of all military personnel, including those who are serving overseas. It provides detailed updates on operations, support and assurance and acts as a complementary service to Military Family Resource Centres.

Family Navigator [www.familynavigator.ca]

Offers toolkits to support CAF families in managing the challenges that come with military life. Includes support for members in caring for a special needs child, elder care, operational injuries, relocation, navigating mental health services, childcare resources, or general information.

Integrated Personnel Support Centres (IPSC)
[www.veterans.gc.ca/eng/services/information-for/caf/ipsc]

With sites across Canada, and in partnership with CAF Health Services, Military Family Services, Operational Stress Injury, Income Security, Personal Support Program and Veterans Affairs Canada, IPSC coordinates core services in the following areas: transition planning, casualty tracking, outreach, advocacy, return to duty and support to CAF families.

Military Families Services [www.familyforce.ca]

Assists families of CAF members in managing the stresses associated with military life through personal, family and community development. In addition, this service encourages participation in the ongoing development and assessment of services for military families. Programs and services include:

Children and Youth
- National Youth Model: provides youth ages 12 to 18 with access to relevant programs and services wherever their families are posted; leadership mentorship

- iSTEP program: 10-week peer-support program for children between the ages of 6 and 12 who have a parent suffering from, or affected by, an operational stress injury

- Children's Deployment Support Program: kid-friendly videos with accompanying scripts on deployment and its impact

- Parent/caregiver education and support, emergency respite care, and child care

Family Separation and Reunion
- Provides outreach, information, and resources to help families cope with deployment, homecoming, and/or injuries.

Education and Training
- Manages overseas schools information to ensure children of CAF personnel receive the same quality of education regardless of the country to which they are posted.

Employment Assistance
- Lists job opportunities at the various bases that are open to family members. Provides updated information on national and regional employment initiatives.

Health Care and Well-Being
- Operation Family Doctor: helps military families find a doctor
- Self-help groups

VETS Canada (Veterans Emergency Transition Services) [http://vetscanada.org/]

Seeks out homeless and at-risk veterans and re-establishes a bond of trust. Helps move them from streets and shelters to affordable housing as well as find suitable employment.

Wounded Warriors [www.woundedwarriors.ca]

Provides a spectrum of mental health support and care for CAF veterans, with a special focus on PTSD. Helps any veteran in need as they transition to civilian life.

Education and Training

This section lists the key providers of services/programs to help CAF transitioning members and veterans determine and secure the education and training needed to prepare for civilian careers.

Algonquin College [www.algonquincollege.com/military]

Algonquin provides credit recognition for the following military occupations:

- CAF Management support clerk
- CAF Basic Military Qualification
  (New Defence and Security Certificate Program)
- CAF Geomatics technician
- CAF Military Police

Algonquin also offers:

- a Subsidized Education Plan for non-commissioned members that pays for all education and training costs while they are in school and provides a guaranteed job upon graduation[75]

- the Project Hero program that provides free tuition to children of CAF soldiers killed in active service.

Athabasca University [www.athabascau.ca]

Athabasca University will accept transfer credits for military experience so that a student can reduce the number of courses required to receive an Athabasca degree. Military members must first apply and be accepted to Athabasca and must have their military experience evaluated by the Military Support Office at the University of Manitoba. The approved credits will, where possible, be applied to the student's program.

British Columbia Institute of Technology (BCIT) Legion Military Skills Conversion Program [www.bcit.ca/legion]

The Legion Military Skills Conversion Program is open to both former and current members of the CAF Regular and Reserve Forces plus the National Guard. Enrolled students can

- fast-track their education by earning BCIT credits in degree/diploma programs such as HR, Operations Management, Business Operations, GIS, Construction, Business Information Technology, and more;

- explore entrepreneurship through the Legion Lions' Lair or the Mindworks programs;

- obtain job-finding and employment assistance dealing with military to civilian skills translation,[76] writing resumés and cover letters, and self-assessment, as well as access to the workbook *Essential Guide to the Civilian Workforce.*

Centennial College (New Business Start-up Program) [www.centennialcollege.ca/coe]

CAF veterans interested in starting their own business can register for the New Business Start-up Program at Centennial College. Offered by the Centre for Entrepreneurship, and boasting a 95% business success rate, the online New Business Start-up Program teaches participants how to develop, refine and implement a business plan. Courses include: assessing demand for your business idea, budget planning, business taxes, business communication, government contracts/tenders, and more. Interested CAF members can consult their Personnel Selection Officer for more information.

Fanshawe College [www.fanshawec.ca]

Fanshawe is a member of a consortium of schools (which includes BCIT, NAIT, Marine Institute of Memorial University and triOS College) that have joined with Canada Company to establish educational pathways whereby those with military training and experience can obtain prior learning credit based on both the schools' and provincial guidelines.

Memorial University of Newfoundland (MUN)

Memorial University is one of the schools that hosts the Based in Business week-long boot camps where transitioning military members can learn the basics of entrepreneurship. Business Administration faculty teach entrepreneurship basics, local business professionals provide real-life business advice, and student volunteers from the Enactus Program (formerly Students in Free Enterprise), provide one-on-one coaching to help participants develop their business idea. Information on Based in Business at MUN: www.business.mun.ca/news-and-highlights/featured-stories/based-in-business-2014.php. Based in Business is run by Prince's Operation Entrepreneur.

Northern Alberta Institute of Technology (NAIT)
[www.nait.ca/canadian-forces-program.htm]

NAIT has a Canadian Forces Program that allows CAF personnel access to a variety of courses, upgrading options and full-time programs. NAIT grants advance credits to CAF members trained in over 13 distinct occupational areas, including Aerospace Telecommunications, Cook, Marine Engineer, Resource Management Clerk, Weapons Technician, and Military Leadership. NAIT also provides a CAF Program Coordinator.

Ottawa Carleton E-School and Canada eSchool
[https://canadaeschool.ca/new-students/miltary-families/]

Offers internet-based high school courses approved by the Ontario Ministry of Education. Provides for the challenges that secondary-school-age children of military members face due to frequent family relocations, credit transfers, or loss of credits due to differing educational requirements.

Trade Certification
[http://www.red-seal.ca/contact/pt-eng.html]

Former CAF military personnel with experience in skilled trades such as plumber, cook, automotive service technician, electrician, carpentry, welder, refrigeration, heavy-duty equipment operator, and more can apply to write provincial or territorial exams to receive Red Seal certification. Two examples:

- **Ontario College of Trades** [www.collegeoftrades. ca/veterans] (Offers the conversion of nine military trade qualifications to civilian trade certification (Red Seal). Fees for the equivalent of a prior learning assessment range from $25 to $200.)

- **Saskatchewan Apprenticeship and Trade Certification Commission** [http://saskapprenticeship.ca/workers/experienced-workers/former-canadian-military-personnel/]

University of Manitoba, Military Support Office [http://umanitoba.ca/faculties/coned/military]

Launched in 1974, the University of Manitoba's Military Support Office recognizes and facilitates the training, mobility and deployment of military personnel. In partnership with DND, the university

- Provides degree credit for specifically evaluated military courses and training

- Oversees a reduced residency requirement for selected degree programs

- Authorizes withdrawals and/or tuition reimbursement if/when military duty conflicts with courses

- Provides academic advising and degree program planning

- Provides support in responding to the educational needs of CAF personnel

Military members can enter their Military Occupational Classification (MOC) and their level of training into the university's Military Credit Transfer Database (http://umanitoba.ca/extended/military/credit) to determine (unofficially) if they are eligible for credits. They can submit their Member Personnel Record Resume (MPRR) and transcripts from other post-secondary institutions to receive an official assessment of transfer credits at no cost.

University of New Brunswick (UNB)
[www.unb.ca/cel/military/credit.html]

UNB will assess military training for possible credit to any of its programs. Applicants need to provide their MPRR (Member Personnel Record Resume), course reports for language training, relevant transcripts and course descriptions, a completed UNB application for admission and pay a fee. UNB also offers Prior Learning Assessment (PLA).

Veteran Transition Network
[www.vtncanada.org]

In this group-based program at the University of British Columbia, transitioning veterans spend 3 weekends over 3 months (80 hours in total) living with and helping each other identify and deal with barriers that hinder their transition to civilian life. In addition to learning communication skills, dealing with trauma, and making psychosocial re-connections, there is a segment dealing with career exploration.

Research

Ongoing research is vital to the development of appropriate services and programs for CAF veterans.

Canadian Institute for Military and Veteran Health Research [https://cimvhr.ca]

This is a consortium of over 30 Canadian universities actively engaged in research on the health needs of military personnel, veterans and their families in order to enhance their lives.

Life After Service Studies (LASS) [www.veterans.gc.ca/ eng/about-us/research-directorate/publications/ reports/2013-life-after-service-studies]

The Life After Service Studies (LASS) program of research is designed to further understand the transition from military to civilian life and ultimately improve the health of veterans in Canada. LASS partners are Veterans Affairs Canada, the Department of National Defence/Canadian Armed Forces Morale and Welfare Services—Publications and Research, and Statistics Canada.

Military Family Services Research [www.cfmws.com/ en/AboutUs/MFS/FamilyResearch/Pages/default.aspx]

From this web page, you can download numerous research papers and publications about military families.

New Initiatives

The CAF, working in partnership with other organizations or government services, is continually exploring and developing resources or programs to better meet the identified career and educational needs of CAF members and veterans. Below are a few of these initiatives.

Canadian Franchise Association, Military Veterans Program [http://lookforafranchise.ca/cfa-military-veterans-program/]

The Canadian Franchise Association in association with the CAF has launched a program specifically for transitioning military members interested in becoming franchise owners. Participating franchises are committed to offering qualified veterans their best offer. As of March 2015, there were over 44 participating franchises and the program is growing.

Career Pathways Catalogue

A catalogue of career-bridging courses, to be offered at reduced cost to military members, veterans and their families over short timeframes, online. Working with the assumption that military members have many core competencies but may lack experience in specific civilian occupations, the pathways will prepare members and veterans for, and assist with, actual job placement. Developers are working closely with industry to ensure that the training provided is directly linked to what industry is seeking. This project is still in development with a first edition comprising 20 distinct career pathways set to launch in January 2016.

CORE Fundamentals

The CORE Fundamentals Program is a high-energy, hands-on workshop designed to equip transitioning service members with personalized guidance and resources to identify and obtain their ideal career in the civilian workforce. Contact core@deloitte.ca for more information.

IBM i2 training

CAF is partnering with IBM Canada to offer training and certification in the i2 Analyst Notebook tool through IBM's Veterans Accelerator Training Program. Trialed in the US and UK, the Accelerator Training program is now available to transitioning CAF members and honourably released veterans. The i2 Analyst Notebook is used by militaries, law enforcement, public safety organizations and private sector companies for intelligence, crime, fraud and cyber security analysis purposes. The CAF and government of Canada agencies are key i2 users.

Shaping Purpose [shapingpurpose.com]

The Shaping Purpose program ran a pilot project, started in April 2015, to help CAF members and veterans identify core gifts, passions and values (GPVs) and thus find the clarity they need to plan their transition to civilian life. Moving forward, four more sessions will be offered (20 soldiers/veterans per session) after which the program will be evaluated. Research outcomes will also be examined following the pilot.

US Resources (Selected List)

There is a wealth of resources available in the United States related to veteran services. Bear in mind, however, that while there are commonalities in needs amongst veterans in general there are distinct differences between CAF and US soldiers. Below is a selected listing of US resources that can broaden understanding of these commonalities.

Career Development for Transitioning Veterans by Carmen Stein-McCormick, Debra S. Osborn, McCoy C.W. Hayden & Dan Van Hoose (National Career Development Association, 2013) [www.ncda.org/aws/NCDA/pt/sd/product/1132/_self/layout_details/false#sthash.fswIGAD8.dpuf.]

This book is geared to career practitioners and is meant to enhance awareness of the transition issues faced by veterans along with the resources available. The book also provides case study examples of how a practitioner might help a veteran through the career planning process.

Credentialing Opportunities On-Line (COOL) [https://www.cool.army.mil/]

Credentialing Opportunities On-Line (COOL) helps US Army soldiers find information on certifications and licenses related to their Military Occupational Specialties (MOSs). It explains how soldiers can meet civilian certification and license requirements and provides links to numerous resources to help get them started. This site also has information for educators and career counsellors on career requirements and work opportunities; can be used by army recruiters to showcase the professional growth and civilian career prep available through service; and can be used by employers and credentialing boards as it showcases how military training and experience prepares soldiers for civilian credentials and jobs. (Note: Soldiers, not Officers, are the focus of this resource.)

G.I. Jobs [www.gijobs.com]

This resource lists military-friendly employers in the US and includes a school matchmaker tool, a job finder, a pay calculator and information on hot jobs for veterans. The section on Getting Out includes a Transition Readiness Quiz.

Global Career Development Facilitators (GCDF) [www.cce-global.org/GCDF]

Offered through the Center for Credentialing & Education, GCDF training allows participants to complete 120 hours of course work as well as work alongside experienced career development professionals in order to learn the skills required to provide career facilitation and guidance. The curriculum is infused with general and country-specific activities and is for veterans who, in their next career, want to help their peers.

Hire Our Heroes [http://hireourheroes.org]

This is a non-profit organization founded and operated by veterans. Its goal is to develop a national approach aimed at reducing the unemployment rate of veterans by reaching out to transitioning veterans within a year prior to discharge. Hire Our Heroes offers training, mentorship and job coaching for veterans as well as dedicated outreach to employers.

Institute for Veterans and Military Families (IVMF) [www.vets.syr.edu]

Housed at Syracuse University, the Institute for Veteran and Military Families collaborates with industry, government, non-governmental organizations and veterans to create education and employment programs to meet the needs of US vets and their families. IVMF provides extensive information/resources for employers and veterans alike.

Military.com [www.military.com]

The Skills Translator on this website (www.military.com/veteran-jobs/skills-translator) helps US service members and veterans translate their military occupations, collateral duties, military training, and day-to-day leadership responsibilities into terms that can be easily understood by a civilian employer. The translator returns civilian job postings matching the veteran's skill profile. This site also has great resumé tips (www.military.com/veteran-jobs/career-advice/resume-writing-archive).

National Career Development Association [www.ncda.org/aws/NCDA/pt/sp/resources]

Provides a list of military resources pertaining to career information, career assessment instruments, professional development and associations. Select "Military" from the Internet Sites for Career Planning menu to access these resources.

O*NET Online [www.onetonline.org]

Similar to the Canadian NOC (National Occupational Classification), this is the primary source for occupational information in the US. It includes a database of occupations, career exploration tools, and assessment tools for finding/changing careers. My Next Move for Veterans (www.mynextmove.org/vets/) is a component of O*NET where US vets can find civilian career matches for their military occupation.

Quintessential Careers [http://www.quintcareers.com/former-military/]

Resources, job search tools, and resumé samples for former military personnel.

RAND Report [www.rand.org/pubs/research_reports/RR836.html]

A comprehensive report on veteran employment in the US and the 100,000 Jobs Mission.

Resume Engine [www.Resumeengine.org]

Developed by the US Chamber of Commerce Foundation and Toyota, this resource is described as the next-generation military skills translator. It allows service members to translate the skills gained during their years of service into language civilian employers can understand. The site also links to a resource for military spouses, Career Spark: www.mycareerspark.org.

Veterans and Military Occupations Finder (VMOF)
[www.self-directed-search.com]

Click on Military and Veterans to access this online resource based on the Self-Directed Search® (SDS). VMOF lists active Military Occupational Classifications from each of the five branches of the US military—Air Force, Army, Coast Guard, Marines, and Navy—along with their corresponding civilian occupations and two-letter Holland Codes. Using these two classifications, users can better understand how they might apply the skills and abilities developed while in the military to civilian occupations with similar requirements.

* * *

"Transition in the Canadian Armed Forces"
is a 12-minute video that addresses the
challenges of transition and offers advice
to those looking to transition:

www.forces.gc.ca/en/caf-community-
health-services/mental-health-in-the-
canadian-armed-forces.page

*Each veteran is a unique individual
and we must approach each ...
with a sense of wonder and awe.*

–Richard N. Bolles[77]

Where to Go From Here

Military to Civilian Employment: A Career Practitioner's Guide provided a broad overview of the military-to-civilian-employment transition. Hopefully what came through in the many lists, links, questions and information provided is that though the transition can be challenging, it can be managed—with preparation, planning, information, support and resources.

Throughout the process of research and writing, the component that continues to resonate the most are the stories of the military members I interviewed. It is therefore fitting that we end this book by giving the last word to heroes Raymond, Emily, Natalie, Marc, Sasha, Kathleen, and McCoy.

What did their stories tell us?

What our storytellers missed most on leaving military service was the camaraderie, team, support, and "feeling of belonging." These came up over and over again—even from Kathleen, our military spouse.

The CAF provides an extremely supportive environment for its members. Whether release was voluntary or involuntary, it is important that career practitioners not overlook how this loss will factor into the adjustment of the military client to civilian life. And while it is true that any individual who has worked in an organization for a long time will require a period of adjustment, it is not often that a group of dissimilar workers will admit to missing the same thing.

Military service also provides its members with a sense of importance. Marc's story in particular bears this out. Outside of the military he feels lost—like a nobody!

Military service gives its members a wealth of opportunities to face and manage challenges. Career practitioners working with military clients can leverage this ability. Yes, the transition to civilian life can be tough. Yes, there might be unexpected hurdles to jump through. But they've faced challenges before and they can do it again—with support.

The advice from our storytellers to those considering the transition was candid and to the point:

- "There is work out there. Wait for a good fit and be prepared to move to find it."

- "Getting it right the first time out of the gate is difficult and not realistic."

- "Spend the time before you leave to figure out what you want."

- "Education is the key in negotiating civilian salary and promotions."

- "You need to bring actual skills to the table."

- "Do a lot of research beforehand; prepare in advance."

- "De-militarize how you speak and communicate."

- "Network long before you decide to leave."

- "Be realistic."

- "Know what you need to do before you jump."

- "Take inventory of your contacts and leverage any connection you can."

In a nutshell, our storytellers repeat the same thing: preparation, patience and people (networks) are the key drivers to successful transitions.

But there is a need for something else.

Transitioning military members need people who understand where they're coming from. People who will help them figure out what they want to do. People who can provide practical support and counsel. People who can help in finding jobs and dealing with barriers.

That's what career practitioners do. That's why our work with transitioning military members is so vitally needed.

How easy it would be to create a forum whereby like-minded career professionals could meet and learn from each other! A yearly meet-up at one of our national conferences, relevant conference presentations, workshops, webinars, a LinkedIn group—these are simple ways to do just that, to add to our learning and broaden our expertise.

Career practitioners can also work to address the need for a more robust Canadian equivalent to the VMOF, building on the work begun in translating MOCs to NOCs. Creating a national standard to aid academic institutions in assessing and crediting military training and experience might be outside our sphere of influence, but we can add our voices and pens to the effort as often as we get the opportunity.[78]

That's where we go from here.

If nothing else, these few actions can help us better serve those who have already served. To them we owe a debt of gratitude.

Bibliography

Anderson, Mary L. and Jane Goodman. "Career Counseling Strategies and Challenges for Transitioning Veterans." *Career Planning and Adult Development Journal* 30, no. 3 (Fall 2014): 40–51.

Anderson, Mary L., Jane Goodman, and Nancy K. Schlossberg. *Counseling Adults in Transition*, 4th ed. New York: Springer Publishing Company, 2011.

Bolles, Richard N. "A Serious Call for More Career Development 'Mechanics' Who Can Help Returning Vets." *Career Planning and Adult Development Journal* 30, no. 3 (Fall 2014): 28–36.

Bolles, Richard N. *What Color is Your Parachute?* 2015 ed. Berkeley: Ten Speed Press, 2014.

Buzzetta, Mary, and Shirley Rowe. "Today's Veterans: Using Cognitive Information Processing (CIP) Approach to Build Upon their Career Dreams." *Career Convergence Magazine*, November 1, 2012. Retrieved from http://www.ncda.org/aws/NCDA/pt/sd/news_article/66290/_self/CC_layout_details/false.

Daigle, Pierre. *On the Homefront: Assessing the Well-being of Canada's Military Families in the New Millennium.* DND/CAF Ombudsman, Special Report to the Minister of National Defence. November 2013. www.ombudsman.forces.gc.ca/en/ombudsman-reports-stats-investigations-military-families/military-families-index.page.

Dallaire, Roméo A. and David M. Wells. *The Transition to Civilian Life of Veterans.* Senate Subcommittee on Veterans Affairs. June 2014. www.parl.gc.ca/Content/SEN/Committee/412/veac/rms/01jun14/Home-e.htm.

Dunn, Jason, Samantha Urban, and Zhigang Wang. "Spousal Employment Income of Canadian Forces Personnel: A Comparison of Civilian Spouses." Findings from Phase II of the Spousal/Partner Employment and Income (SPEI) Project, Director General Military Personnel Research and Analysis, DND. Article available here: www.cfmws.com/en/AboutUs/MFS/FamilyResearch/Pages.

Gaither, Dick. "Military Transition Management." *Career Planning and Adult Development Journal* 30, no. 3 (Fall 2014): 215–39.

Goldfarb, Robert W. "Veterans Battle for Jobs on the Home Front." New York Times, May 9, 2015. www.nytimes.com/2015/05/10/jobs/veterans-battle-for-jobs-on-the-home-front.html.

Hansen, Randall S. "Do's and Don'ts for How to Create Your Military-to-Civilian Transition Resume." Quintessential Careers. http://www.quintcareers.com/military-transition-resume-dos-donts/.

Kurzynski, Krysta. "Veteran Services in Higher Education: Going Above and Beyond." *Career Planning and Adult Development Journal* 30, no. 3 (Fall 2014): 180–90.

Mallen, Sean. "Veterans Face Challenge Finding Civilian Jobs." Global News. November 11, 2014. http://globalnews.ca/news/1666004/veterans-face-challenges-finding-civilian-jobs.

McBride, Pamela, and Lori Cleymans. "A Paradigm Shift: Strategies for Assisting Military Spouses in Obtaining a Successful Career Path." *Career Planning and Adult Development Journal* 30, no. 3 (Fall 2014): 92–102.

Messer, Melissa, and Jennifer Greene. "Development of the Veterans and Military Occupations Finder (VMOF): A New Career Counseling Tool for Veterans and Military Personnel." *Career Planning and Adult Development Journal* 30, no. 3 (Fall 2014): 136–53.

Miles, Robert A. "Career Counseling Strategies and Challenges for Transitioning Veterans." *Career Planning and Adult Development Journal* 30, no. 3 (Fall 2014): 123–35.

Prenzel, Audrey. *Military to Civvie Street*. 2014. E-book available from www.resumeresources.ca.

Reardon, Robert C., Janet G. Lenz, James P. Sampson, and Gary W. Peterson. *Career Development and Planning: A Comprehensive Approach.* 2nd ed. (Custom Publishing, 2005).

Robertson, Heather, Robert A. Miles, and Michelle Mallen. "Career Transition and Military Veterans: An Overview of the Literature from 2000 to 2013." *Career Planning and Adult Development Journal* 30, no. 3 (Fall 2014): 14–27.

Visser, Coert and Gwenda Schlundt Bodien. "Solution-focused Coaching: Simply Effective." 2002. http://articlescoertvisser. blogspot.ca/2007/11/solution-focused-coaching-simply.html.

Military to Civilian Trades

Civilian	MilTrade	MilCategory	MilNCM/ Officer
Accommodation Services Manager	Steward	Air & Ship's Crew	NCM
Accounting Clerk	Resource Management Support Clerk	Administration & Support	NCM
Administrative Services Manager	Steward	Air & Ship's Crew	NCM
Administrative/Financial Clerk	Resource Management Support Clerk	Administration & Support	NCM
Administrator	Intelligence Operator	Other	NCM
Aerospace Engineer	Aerospace Engineering Officer	Engineers	Officer
Air Conditioner Repair Technician	Electronic-Optronic Technician - Land	Technicians	NCM
Air Traffic Controller	Aerospace Control Operator	Sensor & Radar	NCM
Air Traffic Controller	Aerospace Control Officer	Sensor & Radar	Officer
Airborne Radar Operator	Airborne Electronic Sensor Operator	Sensor & Radar	NCM
Airborne Survey Operator	Airborne Electronic Sensor Operator	Sensor & Radar	NCM
Aircraft Maintenance Engineer Avionics (AME-E)	Avionics Systems Technician	Technicians	NCM
Aircraft Maintenance Engineer Mechanical (AME-M)	Aviation Systems Technician	Technicians	NCM
Aircraft Mechanics and Aircraft Inspectors	Air Weapons System Technician	Technicians	NCM
Airline, Corporate Jet or Helicopter Pilot	Pilot	Air & Ship's Crew	Officer
Airport Duty Manager	Aerospace Control Officer	Sensor & Radar	Officer
Airport Fire Fighter	Fire Fighter	Public Protection	NCM
Airport Manager	Aerospace Control Officer	Sensor & Radar	Officer
Ambulance and First Aid Attendant	Medical Technician	Health Care	NCM
Ambulance Attendant and Paramedic	Search and Rescue Technician	Public Protection	NCM
Ambulance Driver	Medical Technician	Health Care	NCM

Civilian	MilTrade	MilCategory	MilNCM/ Officer
Animal Health Technologist	Medical Laboratory Technologist	Health Care	NCM
Appliance Repair Technician	Electrical Distribution Technician	Technicians	NCM
Appliance Service and Repair	Weapons Engineering Technician	Technicians	NCM
Arc/Acetylene Welder	Hull Technician	Technicians	NCM
Architect	Engineering Officer	Engineers	Officer
Arranger or Composer	Musician	Other	NCM
Assembler-Electronic Equipment	Electronic-Optronic Technician - Land	Technicians	NCM
Attendant in Accommodation and Travel	Steward	Air & Ship's Crew	NCM
Audio and Video Recording Technician	Imagery Technician	Other	NCM
Autobody Repair Technician	Materials Technician	Technicians	NCM
Automated-Processing Repair Technician	Electronic-Optronic Technician - Land	Technicians	NCM
Automotive Brake and Front-end Mechanic	Vehicle Technician	Technicians	NCM
Band or Orchestra Leader	Musician	Other	NCM
Banking and Insurance Clerk	Resource Management Support Clerk	Administration & Support	NCM
Biochemistry Technologist	Medical Laboratory Technologist	Health Care	NCM
Biomedical Engineering Technologist	Biomedical Electronics Technologist	Health Care	NCM
Blaster (Construction)	Combat Engineer	Engineers	NCM
Bookkeeper	Resource Management Support Clerk	Administration & Support	NCM
Bookkeeper	Steward	Air & Ship's Crew	NCM
Bus Driver	Mobile Support Equipment Operator	Administration & Support	NCM
Business Administrator	Aerospace Engineering Officer	Engineers	Officer
Business Services Manager	Resource Management Support Clerk	Administration & Support	NCM
Canadian Aviation Maintenance Council (CAMC) Aircraft Maintenance Technician	Aviation Systems Technician	Technicians	NCM
Canadian Aviation Maintenance Council (CAMC) Avionics Maintenance Technician	Avionics Systems Technician	Technicians	NCM
Cargo Agent (Air, Rail, Land and Sea)	Traffic Technician	Administration & Support	NCM
Carpenter	Construction Technician	Technicians	NCM
Carpenter (Rough)	Combat Engineer	Engineers	NCM

Civilian	MilTrade	MilCategory	MilNCM/Officer
Cartographer	Geomatics Technician	Technicians	NCM
Cartographer	Construction Engineering Officer	Engineers	Officer
Certified Engineering Technician (Civil/Construction)	Construction Technician	Technicians	NCM
Certified Engineering Technician (Civil/Construction)	Plumbing and Heating Technician	Technicians	NCM
Certified Engineering Technician (Electrical)	Electrical Distribution Technician	Technicians	NCM
Certified Engineering Technician (Mechanical)	Refrigeration and Mechanical Systems Technician	Technicians	NCM
Certified Engineering Technician (Mechanical)	Water, Fuels and Environmental Technician	Technicians	NCM
Certified Engineering Technician (Mechanical/Electrical)	Electrical Generating Systems Technician	Technicians	NCM
Chauffeur	Mobile Support Equipment Operator	Administration & Support	NCM
Chemical Engineer	Electrical and Mechanical Engineering Officer	Engineers	Officer
Church Headquarters	Chaplain	Other	Officer
Civil Engineering Technician	Combat Engineer	Engineers	NCM
Civilian Ammunition Technician	Ammunition Technician	Technicians	NCM
Columnist	Public Affairs Officer	Administration & Support	Officer
Computer Engineer	Electrical and Mechanical Engineering Officer	Engineers	Officer
Computer Incident Response Specialist	Communicator Research Operator	Telecommunications	NCM
Computer Network or Systems Administrator	Naval Communicator	Telecommunications	NCM
Computer Operator	Armoured Soldier	Combat Specialists	NCM
Computer Operator	Artillery Soldier - Field	Combat Specialists	NCM
Construction Engineer	Construction Engineering Officer	Engineers	Officer
Construction Engineer	Engineering Officer	Engineers	Officer
Construction Engineering Technician	Combat Engineer	Engineers	NCM
Construction Millwright	Combat Engineer	Engineers	NCM
Construction Millwright and Industrial Mechanic	Marine Engineer	Technicians	NCM
Contract Administrator	Supply Technician	Administration & Support	NCM
Correction Services Chaplaincy	Chaplain	Other	Officer
Cryptographer	Naval Communicator	Telecommunications	NCM

Civilian	MilTrade	MilCategory	MilNCM/ Officer
Customer Service, Information Clerk	Resource Management Support Clerk	Administration & Support	NCM
Customs Agent	Traffic Technician	Administration & Support	NCM
Data Base Manager	Geomatics Technician	Technicians	NCM
Data Entry Clerk	Resource Management Support Clerk	Administration & Support	NCM
Deck Hand – Fishing Vessel	Boatswain	Air & Ship's Crew	NCM
Dental Assistant	Dental Technician	Health Care	NCM
Dental Hygienist	Dental Technician	Health Care	NCM
Dentist	Dental Officer	Health Care	Officer
Diagnostic Ultrasound Technologist	Medical Radiation Technologist	Health Care	NCM
Director of Public Works	Construction Engineering Officer	Engineers	Officer
Director, Public Relations	Public Affairs Officer	Administration & Support	Officer
Dispatcher and Radiotelephone Operator	Naval Combat Information Operator	Engineers	NCM
Dispatcher, Motor Vehicles	Mobile Support Equipment Operator	Administration & Support	NCM
Driver	Artillery Soldier - Field	Combat Specialists	NCM
Drywaller/Plasterer	Construction Technician	Technicians	NCM
Ecumenical Organizations	Chaplain	Other	Officer
Editor, News and Special Events	Public Affairs Officer	Administration & Support	Officer
Electric Truck Servicer (Forklifts)	Electronic-Optronic Technician - Land	Technicians	NCM
Electrical & Electronic Engineering Technologists & Technicians	Air Weapons System Technician	Technicians	NCM
Electrical and Electronics Engineer	Weapons Engineering Technician	Technicians	NCM
Electrical and Electronics Engineers	Electrical and Mechanical Engineering Officer	Engineers	Officer
Electrician	Electrical Distribution Technician	Technicians	NCM
Electrician Apprentice	Electrical Technician	Technicians	NCM
Electrician Helper (Shipboard)	Electrical Technician	Technicians	NCM
Electrician Helper (Shipboard)	Weapons Engineering Technician	Technicians	NCM
Electrician Power Line and Cable Worker	Electrical Distribution Technician	Technicians	NCM
Electrician Repairman Helper	Electrical Technician	Technicians	NCM

Civilian	MilTrade	MilCategory	MilNCM/Officer
Electrician, Marine Equipment	Electrical Technician	Technicians	NCM
Electro-Mechanical Technician	Electronic-Optronic Technician - Land	Technicians	NCM
Electronic Engineering Technician	Aerospace Telecommunication & Information Systems Technician	Telecommunications	NCM
Electronic Engineering Technician/Technologist	Army Communication and Information Systems Specialist	Telecommunications	NCM
Electronic Engineering Technician/Technologist	Electronic-Optronic Technician - Land	Technicians	NCM
Electronic Engineering Technologist	Aerospace Telecommunication & Information Systems Technician	Telecommunications	NCM
Electronic Service Technician	Aerospace Telecommunication & Information Systems Technician	Telecommunications	NCM
Electronics Repair Apprentice	Weapons Engineering Technician	Technicians	NCM
Electronics Repair Journeyman	Weapons Engineering Technician	Technicians	NCM
Emergency Medical Attendant (EMA)	Medical Technician	Health Care	NCM
Emerging Science and Technical Fields	Electrical and Mechanical Engineering Officer	Engineers	Officer
Employment Supervisor	Personnel Selection Officer	Administration & Support	Officer
Engineering Inspectors and Regulatory	Ammunition Technician	Technicians	NCM
Environmental Assessor	Water, Fuels and Environmental Technician	Technicians	NCM
Environmental Engineer	Engineering Officer	Engineers	Officer
Equipment Mechanic	Marine Engineer	Technicians	NCM
Explosive and Ammunitions Magazine Foreman/woman	Air Weapons System Technician	Technicians	NCM
Facilities Manager	Construction Engineering Officer	Engineers	Officer
Facility Operations Manager	Army Communication and Information Systems Specialist	Telecommunications	NCM
Facility Operations Manager	Aerospace Control Officer	Sensor & Radar	Officer
Federal Public Service: Computer Services	Geomatics Technician	Technicians	NCM
Federal Public Service: Engineering and Scientific Support	Geomatics Technician	Technicians	NCM
Fire Alarm Installer and Repairer	Electrical Distribution Technician	Technicians	NCM
Fire Chief	Construction Engineering Officer	Engineers	Officer
Fire Inspector	Fire Fighter	Public Protection	NCM
Fire Instructor	Fire Fighter	Public Protection	NCM
Fire Investigator	Fire Fighter	Public Protection	NCM

Civilian	MilTrade	MilCategory	MilNCM/ Officer
Fire Officer	Fire Fighter	Public Protection	NCM
Firearms Inspector	Weapons Technician	Technicians	NCM
Firefighter	Armoured Soldier	Combat Specialists	NCM
Firefighter	Search and Rescue Technician	Public Protection	NCM
Flight Attendant, Purser	Steward	Air & Ship's Crew	NCM
Flight Instructor (basic through Jets or Helicopters)	Pilot	Air & Ship's Crew	Officer
Flight Line Agent	Traffic Technician	Administration & Support	NCM
Flight Service Specialist	Aerospace Control Officer	Sensor & Radar	Officer
Food Counter Attendant, Kitchen Helper	Steward	Air & Ship's Crew	NCM
Food Service Supervisor	Steward	Air & Ship's Crew	NCM
Food Services Instructor in High Schools or Colleges	Cook	Administration & Support	NCM
Foreign Service Officer	Public Affairs Officer	Administration & Support	Officer
Forestry Technologist and Technician	Search and Rescue Technician	Public Protection	NCM
Gasfitter	Weapons Technician	Technicians	NCM
General Machinist	Materials Technician	Technicians	NCM
General Office Clerk	Resource Management Support Clerk	Administration & Support	NCM
General Welder	Materials Technician	Technicians	NCM
Geodetic Surveyor	Geomatics Technician	Technicians	NCM
Geographic Information System Technician	Geomatics Technician	Technicians	NCM
Geological Engineer	Engineering Officer	Engineers	Officer
Guard	Armoured Soldier	Combat Specialists	NCM
Gun Assembler	Weapons Technician	Technicians	NCM
Gunsmith	Weapons Technician	Technicians	NCM
Hazardous Material Incident Commander	Fire Fighter	Public Protection	NCM
Hazardous Material Technician	Fire Fighter	Public Protection	NCM
Head Bartender and Barkeeper	Steward	Air & Ship's Crew	NCM
Health Care Administrator	Health Care Administration Officer	Administration & Support	Officer

Civilian	MilTrade	MilCategory	MilNCM/Officer
Heating Technician	Plumbing and Heating Technician	Technicians	NCM
Heavy Equipment Operator	Armoured Soldier	Combat Specialists	NCM
Heavy Equipment Operator	Combat Engineer	Engineers	NCM
Heavy-Duty Equipment Mechanic	Marine Engineer	Technicians	NCM
High-Pressure Welder	Materials Technician	Technicians	NCM
Highway Construction Foreman	Combat Engineer	Engineers	NCM
Histology Technologist	Medical Laboratory Technologist	Health Care	NCM
Hospital Administrator	Health Care Administration Officer	Administration & Support	Officer
Hospital Operations Officer	Health Care Administration Officer	Administration & Support	Officer
Hospital Services Officer	Health Care Administration Officer	Administration & Support	Officer
Hospital, School and University Chaplaincies	Chaplain	Other	Officer
Hotel Clerk Supervisor	Steward	Air & Ship's Crew	NCM
Hotel Front Desk Clerk	Steward	Air & Ship's Crew	NCM
Human Resource Manager	Resource Management Support Clerk	Administration & Support	NCM
Human Resources Manager	Aerospace Control Officer	Sensor & Radar	Officer
Human Resources Manager	Aerospace Engineering Officer	Engineers	Officer
Human Resources Manager	Engineering Officer	Engineers	Officer
HVAC Technician	Refrigeration and Mechanical Systems Technician	Technicians	NCM
Hydraulics Technician	Weapons Technician	Technicians	NCM
Hydro Power Station Operator	Marine Engineer	Technicians	NCM
Imagery Specialist	Intelligence Operator	Other	NCM
Imagery Specialist	Intelligence Officer	Other	Officer
Industrial and Manufacturing Engineer	Electrical and Mechanical Engineering Officer	Engineers	Officer
Industrial Electrical Technician	Electrical Generating Systems Technician	Technicians	NCM
Industrial Mechanic	Electrical Generating Systems Technician	Technicians	NCM
Industrial Truck Mechanic	Vehicle Technician	Technicians	NCM
Information Management Specialist	Communicator Research Operator	Telecommunications	NCM

Civilian	MilTrade	MilCategory	MilNCM/Officer
Information Management Specialist	Intelligence Operator	Other	NCM
Information Management Specialist	Intelligence Officer	Other	Officer
Information Systems Analyst	Army Communication and Information Systems Specialist	Telecommunications	NCM
Information Technology Security Consultant	Communicator Research Operator	Telecommunications	NCM
Information Technology Security Consultant	Intelligence Operator	Other	NCM
Information Technology Security Consultant	Intelligence Officer	Other	Officer
Institutional or Restaurant Cook	Cook	Administration & Support	NCM
Instrumental Musician	Musician	Other	NCM
Intelligence Analyst	Communicator Research Operator	Telecommunications	NCM
Intelligence Analyst or Operator	Intelligence Operator	Other	NCM
Intelligence Analyst or Operator	Intelligence Officer	Other	Officer
Invoicing/Auditing Agent	Traffic Technician	Administration & Support	NCM
Journalist	Intelligence Operator	Other	NCM
Journalist	Intelligence Officer	Other	Officer
Judge	Legal Officer	Other	Officer
Junior Manager	Artillery Soldier - Field	Combat Specialists	NCM
Laser Equipment Technician	Electronic-Optronic Technician - Land	Technicians	NCM
Law Enforcement Thermographer	Airborne Electronic Sensor Operator	Sensor & Radar	NCM
Lawyer	Legal Officer	Other	Officer
Library Clerk	Resource Management Support Clerk	Administration & Support	NCM
Licensed Practical Nurse	Medical Technician	Health Care	NCM
Lifeguard	Search and Rescue Technician	Public Protection	NCM
Line Installer-Repairer Technician	Army Communication and Information Systems Specialist	Telecommunications	NCM
Locksmith	Weapons Technician	Technicians	NCM
Machine Operator	Materials Technician	Technicians	NCM
Mail Clerk	Postal Clerk	Administration & Support	NCM
Mail Sorter	Postal Clerk	Administration & Support	NCM

Civilian	MilTrade	MilCategory	MilNCM/Officer
Maître d'hôtel and Host/Hostess	Steward	Air & Ship's Crew	NCM
Manager of a Flight Operations department	Pilot	Air & Ship's Crew	Officer
Manager or Supervisor (Food Service Establishment)	Cook	Administration & Support	NCM
Manpower Counsellor	Personnel Selection Officer	Administration & Support	Officer
Marine Traffic Controller	Naval Communicator	Telecommunications	NCM
Marine Weapons Engineering Technician	Weapons Engineering Technician	Technicians	NCM
Maritime Traffic Controller	Naval Combat Information Operator	Engineers	NCM
Mason	Construction Technician	Technicians	NCM
Material handlers	Ammunition Technician	Technicians	NCM
Material Manager	Supply Technician	Administration & Support	NCM
Mechanical Engineering	Electrical and Mechanical Engineering Officer	Engineers	Officer
Medical Laboratory Technologist	Medical Laboratory Technologist	Health Care	NCM
Medical Laboratory Technologist and Pathologist Assistant	Medical Laboratory Technologist	Health Care	NCM
Medical Radiation Technologist	Medical Radiation Technologist	Health Care	NCM
Medical Supply Clerk	Medical Technician	Health Care	NCM
Metallurgical and Manu-facturing Engineers	Electrical and Mechanical Engineering Officer	Engineers	Officer
Meteorological Inspector	Meteorological Technician	Technicians	NCM
Microbiology Technologist	Medical Laboratory Technologist	Health Care	NCM
Millwright	Hull Technician	Technicians	NCM
Millwright	Materials Technician	Technicians	NCM
Millwright	Weapons Technician	Technicians	NCM
Minilab Operator	Imagery Technician	Other	NCM
Mining Engineer	Engineering Officer	Engineers	Officer
Municipal Engineer	Construction Engineering Officer	Engineers	Officer
News Analyst, Broadcasting	Public Affairs Officer	Administration & Support	Officer
Non-Governmental Organizations	Chaplain	Other	Officer
Nurse	Nursing Officer	Health Care	Officer

Civilian	MilTrade	MilCategory	MilNCM/Officer
Office Manager	Resource Management Support Clerk	Administration & Support	NCM
Operator and Attendant in the Fields of Amusement, Recreation and Sports	Steward	Air & Ship's Crew	NCM
Optical/Optronic Technician	Electronic-Optronic Technician - Land	Technicians	NCM
Oral and Maxillofacial Surgeon	Dental Officer	Health Care	Officer
Other Assemblers and Inspectors	Ammunition Technician	Technicians	NCM
Other Federal Law Enforcement: Customs, Immigration and Fisheries	Military Police	Public Protection	NCM
Other Federal Law Enforcement: Customs, Immigration and Fisheries	Military Police Officer	Public Protection	Officer
Other Metal Products Machine Operators	Ammunition Technician	Technicians	NCM
Other Professional Engineers	Electrical and Mechanical Engineering Officer	Engineers	Officer
Outdoor Sport and Recreational Guide	Search and Rescue Technician	Public Protection	NCM
Painter/Glazier	Construction Technician	Technicians	NCM
Painter–Spray Finisher	Materials Technician	Technicians	NCM
Paralegal	Intelligence Operator	Other	NCM
Pastoral Counselling Education	Chaplain	Other	Officer
Payroll Clerk	Resource Management Support Clerk	Administration & Support	NCM
PC Service Technician	Aerospace Telecommunication & Information Systems Technician	Telecommunications	NCM
Periodontist	Dental Officer	Health Care	Officer
Personnel and Recruitment Officer	Resource Management Support Clerk	Administration & Support	NCM
Personnel Clerk	Resource Management Support Clerk	Administration & Support	NCM
Personnel Officer	Personnel Selection Officer	Administration & Support	Officer
Petroleum Engineer	Electrical and Mechanical Engineering Officer	Engineers	Officer
Pharmacist	Pharmacy Officer	Health Care	Officer
Photogrammetrist	Geomatics Technician	Technicians	NCM
Photographers (All types)	Imagery Technician	Other	NCM
Physician	Medical Officer	Health Care	Officer
Physiotherapist	Physiotherapy Officer	Health Care	Officer
Plumber	Hull Technician	Technicians	NCM

Civilian	MilTrade	MilCategory	MilNCM/Officer
Plumber	Plumbing and Heating Technician	Technicians	NCM
Police and Security Investigator and Consultant	Intelligence Officer	Other	Officer
Political Analyst	Intelligence Officer	Other	Officer
Political Scientist and Theorist	Intelligence Officer	Other	Officer
Power Plant Operator	Electrical Generating Systems Technician	Technicians	NCM
Primary Care Paramedic	Medical Technician	Health Care	NCM
Private Investigator	Intelligence Operator	Other	NCM
Professional Church Worker	Chaplain	Other	Officer
Project Manager – Construction	Construction Engineering Officer	Engineers	Officer
Property Administrator	Steward	Air & Ship's Crew	NCM
Prosthodontist	Dental Officer	Health Care	Officer
Provincial, Regional and Municipal Police Services	Military Police	Public Protection	NCM
Provincial, Regional and Municipal Police Services	Military Police Officer	Public Protection	Officer
Psychologist – General, Developmental, Social, Counselling, Industrial or Educational	Personnel Selection Officer	Administration & Support	Officer
Public Health Dentist	Dental Officer	Health Care	Officer
Purchasing Manager	Steward	Air & Ship's Crew	NCM
Purchasing Officer	Supply Technician	Administration & Support	NCM
Radio Communications Equipment Repairer	Aerospace Telecommunication & Information Systems Technician	Telecommunications	NCM
Radio Operator	Naval Communicator	Telecommunications	NCM
Railway and Maritime Controller	Aerospace Control Operator	Sensor & Radar	NCM
Railway and Maritime Traffic Controller	Aerospace Control Officer	Sensor & Radar	Officer
RCMP	Military Police	Public Protection	NCM
RCMP	Military Police Officer	Public Protection	Officer
Realty Asset Manager	Construction Engineering Officer	Engineers	Officer
Records and File Clerk	Resource Management Support Clerk	Administration & Support	NCM
Refrigeration Technician	Refrigeration and Mechanical Systems Technician	Technicians	NCM

Civilian	MilTrade	MilCategory	MilNCM/Officer
Registered Nursing Assistant	Medical Technician	Health Care	NCM
Restaurant and Food Services Manager	Steward	Air & Ship's Crew	NCM
Retail Trade Manager	Steward	Air & Ship's Crew	NCM
Retail Trade Supervisor	Steward	Air & Ship's Crew	NCM
Roofer	Construction Technician	Technicians	NCM
Security Alarm Installer and Maintainer	Electrical Distribution Technician	Technicians	NCM
Security Consultant	Intelligence Operator	Other	NCM
Senior Project Manager - Construction	Engineering Officer	Engineers	Officer
Sheet Metal Worker	Hull Technician	Technicians	NCM
Sheet-Metal Worker	Materials Technician	Technicians	NCM
Ship Carpenter	Hull Technician	Technicians	NCM
Ship's Boatswain	Boatswain	Air & Ship's Crew	NCM
Shipping and Receiving Agent	Traffic Technician	Administration & Support	NCM
Short Order Cook	Steward	Air & Ship's Crew	NCM
Singer	Musician	Other	NCM
Small Arms Tester	Weapons Technician	Technicians	NCM
Snow Removal Equipment Operator	Mobile Support Equipment Operator	Administration & Support	NCM
Special Social Ministries such as Street Ministry	Chaplain	Other	Officer
Staff Officers	Resource Management Support Clerk	Administration & Support	NCM
Stationary Engineer and Auxiliary Equipment Operator	Marine Engineer	Technicians	NCM
Storekeeper and Parts Clerk	Steward	Air & Ship's Crew	NCM
Stores Person	Supply Technician	Administration & Support	NCM
Structural Fire Fighter	Fire Fighter	Public Protection	NCM
Supervisor of Finance and Insurance Clerks	Steward	Air & Ship's Crew	NCM
Surveillance/Thermal Equipment Technician	Electronic-Optronic Technician - Land	Technicians	NCM
Survey Instrument Repairman	Electronic-Optronic Technician - Land	Technicians	NCM
Surveyor	Artillery Soldier - Field	Combat Specialists	NCM

Civilian	MilTrade	MilCategory	MilNCM/Officer
Telecommunication Cabling Network Designer and Manager	Army Communication and Information Systems Specialist	Telecommunications	NCM
Telecommunications Equipment Installer	Aerospace Telecommunication & Information Systems Technician	Telecommunications	NCM
Telecommunications Operator and Manager	Army Communication and Information Systems Specialist	Telecommunications	NCM
Television Repair Technician	Electronic-Optronic Technician - Land	Technicians	NCM
Test/Delivery Pilot for an Aircraft Manufacturer	Pilot	Air & Ship's Crew	Officer
Textile Repair Technician	Materials Technician	Technicians	NCM
Ticket and Cargo Agent	Resource Management Support Clerk	Administration & Support	NCM
Tool-and-Die Maker	Materials Technician	Technicians	NCM
Transport Canada Pilot Inspector	Pilot	Air & Ship's Crew	Officer
Travel Agent	Traffic Technician	Administration & Support	NCM
Truck Driver	Mobile Support Equipment Operator	Administration & Support	NCM
Truck or Forklift Operator	Supply Technician	Administration & Support	NCM
Truck-Trailer Repairer	Vehicle Technician	Technicians	NCM
Tugboat Captain	Boatswain	Air & Ship's Crew	NCM
Tune-up Specialist	Vehicle Technician	Technicians	NCM
Utilities Manager	Construction Engineering Officer	Engineers	Officer
Utilities/Equipment Manager	Engineering Officer	Engineers	Officer
Video Camera Operator	Imagery Technician	Other	NCM
Video Editor	Imagery Technician	Other	NCM
Warehouse Manager	Traffic Technician	Administration & Support	NCM
Warehouse Supervisor	Supply Technician	Administration & Support	NCM
Waste Water Plant Technician	Water, Fuels and Environmental Technician	Technicians	NCM
Water Bomber or Medical Evacuation Pilot	Pilot	Air & Ship's Crew	Officer
Water Plant Technician	Water, Fuels and Environmental Technician	Technicians	NCM
Weather Service Specialist	Meteorological Technician	Technicians	NCM
Youth Ministry	Chaplain	Other	Officer

APPENDIX 2 –

Selected Military Acronyms and Initialisms Used in the Book

CAF	Canadian Armed Forces
CDA	Canadian Defence Academy
CF	Canadian Forces
CFC	Canadian Forces College
CO	Commissioned Officer
CTS	Career Transition Services
DND	Department of National Defence
MILPERSGEN	Military Personnel Generation Formation
MOC	Military Occupation Code
MPRR	Member Personnel Record Resume
NCM	Non-Commissioned Member
RMCC	Royal Military College of Canada
SCAN	Second Career Assistance Network
TOS	Term of Service
VAC	Veterans Affairs Canada
VETS	Veterans Emergency Transition Services

About the Publisher

Military to Civilian Employment: A Career Practitioner's Guide is published by the Canadian Education and Research Institute for Counselling (CERIC), a charitable organization that advances education and research in career counselling and career development in order to increase the economic and social well-being of Canadians.

CERIC funds projects to develop innovative resources that build the knowledge and skills of diverse career professionals. CERIC also hosts Cannexus, Canada's largest annual bilingual career development conference; publishes the country's only peer-reviewed career development journal, *The Canadian Journal of Career Development*; and runs the free ContactPoint / OrientAction online communities, which provide learning and networking in the career field.

CERIC's activities are funded in large part by The Counselling Foundation of Canada, a family foundation that has actively supported career projects for more than 50 years.

Organizational Contributors

The following organizations are major contributors to the content of this guide:

- Canada Company
- Canadian Armed Forces Career Transition Section
- Military Family Services
- Military2civilianemployment.com
- Veterans Affairs Canada

About the Author

Yvonne Rodney works as a career development practitioner, author, playwright, theatre director, women's leader, and fills many other life roles. Published books include *Curse God and Die*, *The Waiting Heart*, *Let it Go*, and *Getting Through*; theatrical productions include the popular *Finding a Wife for Isaiah* and *Something to Offer* staged at the Toronto Centre for the Arts. Yvonne has presented extensively at conferences and business-related events on the topics of career, personal and professional development, and spirituality. She currently presides over Inner Change Consulting (www.innerchangeconsulting.com) and consults part-time with Jewish Vocational Services.

Notes

1   Blake C. Goldring, M.S.M., is founder and chair of Canada Company and Honorary Colonel, Canadian Army.

2   "Definition of a Veteran," Veterans Affairs Canada, last modified March 11, 2015, www.veterans.gc.ca/eng/about-us/definition-veteran.

3   FAQ #12: "How many CAF members and DND employees are there?" www.forces.gc.ca/en/about/faq.page.

4   Information taken from "About the Canadian Armed Forces": www.forces.gc.ca/en/about/canadian-armed-forces.page.

5   Rangers provide "patrols and detachments for national-security and public-safety missions along the northern and coastal areas of Canada not covered by other parts of the CAF." For more information about the Canadian Rangers, see "About the Canadian Rangers," Canadian Army, www.army-armee.forces.gc.ca/en/canadian-rangers/about.page.

Introduction

6   Sean Mallen, "Veterans Face Challenges Finding Civilian Jobs," *Global News*, November 11, 2014, http://globalnews.ca/news/1666004/veterans-face-challenges-finding-civilian-jobs.

7   Roméo A. Dallaire and David M. Wells, Senate Subcommittee on Veterans Affairs, *The Transition to Civilian Life of Veterans*, June 2014, www.parl.gc.ca/Content/SEN/Committee/412/veac/rms/01jun14/Home-e.htm. Note that members who serve in the Reserve Forces have unique employment-related challenges—see Chapter 2, Reservists, and Chapter 4, Working with Reservists: Military Leave.

Part I

8 Blake Goldring, "Looking after the Veterans of Today," *National Post*, November 11, 2013, http://news.nationalpost.com/full-comment/ blake-goldring-looking-after-the-veterans-of-today.

Chapter 1

9 Roméo A. Dallaire and David M. Wells, Senate Subcommittee on Veterans Affairs, *The Transition to Civilian Life of Veterans*, June 2014, www.parl.gc.ca/Content/SEN/Committee/412/veac/rms/01jun14/ Home-e.htm.

10 Melissa Martin, "Military to Civilian Timeline," February 17, 2014, http://military2civilianemployment.com/military-to-civilian-timeline.

11 CERIC, "Transitioning from Military to Civilian Careers: A Career Needs Assessment Report" (unpublished, 2014).

12 Krysta Kurzynski, "Veteran Services in Higher Education: Going Above and Beyond," *Career Planning and Adult Development Journal* 30, no. 3 (Fall 2014): 180–90.

13 As suggested by Robert A. Miles in "Career Counseling Strategies and Challenges for Transitioning Veterans," *Career Planning and Adult Development Journal* 30, no. 3 (Fall 2014): 123–35.

14 Suggestion noted by Heather Robertson, Robert A. Miles, and Michelle Mallen in "Career Transition and Military Veterans: An Overview of the Literature from 2000 to 2013," *Career Planning and Adult Development Journal* 30, no. 3 (Fall 2014): 14–27. For more information on the Global Career Development Facilitators (GCDF) program, visit www.cce-global.org/GCDF.

15 The Universality of Service principle, or "soldier first," holds that CAF members are liable to perform general military duties and common defence and security duties, not just the duties of their military occupation or occupational specification. This may include, but is not limited to, the requirement to be physically fit, employable and deployable for general operational duties. See "Fit to Serve: Universality of Service and Related Support Programs CAF," www. forces.gc.ca/en/news/article.page?doc=fit-to-serve-universality-of-service-and-related-support-programs/hnps1vfl.

16 *Surgeon General's Mental Health Strategy: Canadian Forces Health Services Group – An Evolution of Excellence*, p. 3, www.forces.gc.ca/en/about-reports-pubs-health/surg-gen-mental-health-strategy-toc.page.

17 Standing Committee on Veterans Affairs, Support for Veterans and Other Victims of Post Traumatic Stress Disorder and Other Operational Stress Injuries, 39th Parliament, 1st Session, Report 6, June 2007, www.parl.gc.ca/HousePublications/Publication.aspx?DocId=3042769&Language=E&Mode=1&Parl=39&Ses=1&File=9 "Executive Summary for the Report on Cumulative Incidence of Post-Traumatic Stress Disorder and Other Mental Disorders," Department of National Defence / Canadian Armed Forces, www.forces.gc.ca/en/about-reports-pubs-health/cumulative-incidents-exec-summary.page? .

18 Richard N. Bolles, "A Serious Call for More Career Development 'Mechanics' Who Can Help Returning Vets, *Career Planning and Adult Development Journal* 30, no. 3 (Fall 2014): 28–36.

19 Robert W. Goldfarb, "Veterans Battle for Jobs on the Home Front," *New York Times*, May 9, 2015, www.nytimes.com/2015/05/10/jobs/veterans-battle-for-jobs-on-the-home-front.html.

20 L. Van Til et al, 2013 *Synthesis of Life After Service Studies*, Veterans Affairs Canada, Research Directorate, July 3, 2104, www.veterans.gc.ca/eng/about-us/research-directorate/publications/reports/2013-life-after-service-studies.

21 Richard N. Bolles, "A Serious Call for More Career Development 'Mechanics' Who Can Help Returning Vets, *Career Planning and Adult Development Journal* 30, no. 3 (Fall 2014): 28.

Chapter 2

22 "Joining the Reserves," Canadian Armed Forces, www.forces.ca/en/page/applynow-100#who.

23 Approximately 40 of 51 CAF non-commissioned member (NCM) occupations require Grade 10 math, 5 require completion of high school, and 6 completion of college/Cegep. All commissioned Officer (CO) occupations require a university degree.

24 The DND and CF Code of Values and Ethics consists of three key principles—respect the dignity of all persons, serve Canada before self, and obey and support lawful authority—and five core values—integrity, loyalty, stewardship, courage and excellence—each with clearly outlined behavioural expectations. See "The DND and CF Code of Values and Ethics," www.forces.gc.ca/en/about/code-of-values-and-ethics.page.

25 For details about career options, see www.forces.ca/en/page/careeroptions-123.

26 As noted in Chapter 1, the Universality of Service principle, or "soldier first," holds that CF members are liable to perform general military duties and common defence and security duties, not just the duties of their military occupation or occupational specification. This may include, but is not limited to, the requirement to be physically fit, employable and deployable for general operational duties. See "Fit to Serve: Universality of Service and Related Support Programs CAF," www.forces.gc.ca/en/news/article.page?doc=fit-to-serve-universality-of-service-and-related-support-programs/hnps1vfl.

27 Information provided by the Director, Casualty Support Management, CAF Transition Office, Canadian Armed Forces.

28 Dick Gaither, "Military Transition Management," *Career Planning and Adult Development Journal* 30, no. 3 (Fall 2014): 215–39.

Part II

29 Ron and Caryl Krannich, I Want to Do Something Else, but I'm Not Sure What It Is (Manassas Park, Virginia: Impact, 2005), 79.

Chapter 3

30 For more information on this topic see Diane Hudson Burns, "Understanding How Military and Civilian Cultures Differ," Job-Hunt.org, www.job-hunt.org/veterans-job-search/military-vs-civilian-cultures.shtml.

31 CERIC, "Transitioning from Military to Civilian Careers: A Career Needs Assessment Report" (unpublished, 2014).

32 Robert A. Miles, "Career Counseling Strategies and Challenges for Transitioning Veterans," *Career Planning and Adult Development Journal* 30, no. 3 (Fall 2014): 123–35.

33 Robert W. Goldfarb, "Veterans Battle for Jobs on the Home Front," *New York Times*, May 9, 2015, www.nytimes.com/2015/05/10/jobs/veterans-battle-for-jobs-on-the-home-front.html.

34 Download the Veteran and Military Occupations Finder here: www.self-directed-search.com/docs/default-source/default-document-library/sds_vmof_online_edition.pdf?sfvrsn=2. A word of caution: US occupations can be different than CAF occupations in scope even though they may have similar names. Consult with your client to gain a full understanding of the nature of their work.

35 Robert A. Miles, "Career Counseling Strategies and Challenges for Transitioning Veterans," *Career Planning and Adult Development Journal* 30, no. 3 (Fall 2014): 123–35.

36 CAF job description for an artillery soldier: www.forces.ca/en/job/artillerysoldier-2.

37 Melissa Messer and Jennifer Greene, "Development of the Veterans and Military Occupations Finder (VMOF): A New Career Counseling Tool for Veterans and Military Personnel," *Career Planning and Adult Development Journal* 30, no. 3 (Fall 2014): 136–53.

38 Robertson, Robert A. Miles, and Michelle Mallen, "Career Transition and Military Veterans: An Overview of the Literature from 2000 to 2013," *Career Planning and Adult Development Journal* 30, no. 3 (Fall 2014): 14–27.

39 Dick Gaither, "Military Transition Management," *Career Planning and Adult Development Journal* 30, no. 3 (Fall 2014): 221.

Chapter 4

40 Richard N. Bolles, "A Serious Call for More Career Development 'Mechanics' Who Can Help Returning Vets, *Career Planning and Adult Development Journal* 30, no. 3 (Fall 2014): 28–36.

41 For a discussion of skills translation see Chapter 3, The Difficulty of Articulating and Translating Skills. For a discussion of other tools

to determine see Chapter 3, Not Knowing Civilian Job Equivalents. Two American resources are also worth noting here, with the caveat that US military occupations do not always match CAF occupations directly. Their usefulness is helping CAF clients identify transferable skills and determine Canadian job equivalents is thus limited. (1) The Skills Translator at Military.com: Given an occupational title, environment (Army, Marine, etc.) and pay grade, the Skills Translator will provide a list of civilian skills and a listing of current job postings across the US: www.military.com/veteran-jobs/skills-translator. (2) The Veterans Military Occupations Finder (VMOF) includes a feature called the Military to Civilian Crosswalk whereby one can match military occupations with their civilian equivalent(s) and corresponding Holland Code: www.self-directed-search.com/docs/default-source/default-document-library/sds_vmof_online_edition.pdf?sfvrsn=2.

42 Randall S. Hansen, "Do's and Don'ts for How to Create Your Military-to-Civilian Transition Resume," Quintessential Careers, www.quintcareers.com/military_transition_resume_dos-donts.html.

43 For more information on military resumés see (1) Audrey Prenzel, *Military to Civvie Street* (e-book): www.resumeresources.ca; (2) Resume Engine: www.resumeengine.org; (3) Career, Job, and Entrepreneurial Tools for Transitioning Veterans & Former Military, Quintessential Careers: www.quintcareers.com/former_military.html; (4) Resume Writing Archive, Military.com: www.military.com/veteran-jobs/career-advice/resume-writing-archive.

44 The Veterans Hiring Act came into force July 1, 2015. Details for the human resources community can be found here: "Veterans Hiring Act," Public Service Commission of Canada, www.psc-cfp.gc.ca/plcy-pltq/vet-ac/index-eng.htm.

45 "Career Edge Internship Program for Canadian Reservists," www.careeredge.ca/en/job-seekers/cafreservists.

46 "Job Protection Legislation," Department of National Defence/Canadian Armed Forces, last modified September 12, 2014, www.forces.gc.ca/en/business-reservist-support/job-protection-legislation.page.

47 Sample letters for use by reservists: www.forces.gc.ca/en/business-reservist-support/tools-sample-letters.page.

48 "Meaningful work" is used here to refer to work that not only pays the bills but provides a sense of value and satisfaction.

49 *Military to Civvie Street* is available here: http://www.resumeresources.ca.

Part III

50 Mary L. Anderson, Jane Goodman, Nancy K. Schlossberg, *Counseling Adults in Transition*, 4th ed. (New York: Springer Publishing Company, 2011), 30.

Chapter 5

51 Robert A. Miles, "Career Counseling Strategies and Challenges for Transitioning Veterans," *Career Planning and Adult Development Journal* 30, no. 3 (Fall 2014): 123–35.

52 While our primary focus is on helping our clients in their career development, sometimes it becomes obvious that other personal issues need to be addressed before the client can continue with their career plans. Practitioners who do not have professional training in therapeutic interventions should tactfully discuss this with the client and offer, if needed, referral to an appropriate professional.

53 Mary L. Anderson and Jane Goodman, "Career Counseling Strategies and Challenges for Transitioning Veterans," *Career Planning and Adult Development Journal* 30, no. 3 (Fall 2014): 40–51. For more information on this approach and on transition in general see Mary L. Anderson, Jane Goodman, and Nancy K. Schlossberg, *Counseling Adults in Transition*, 4th ed. (New York: Springer Publishing Company, 2011), 360 pages.

54 Robert C. Reardon, Janet G. Lenz, James P. Sampson, and Gary W. Peterson, *Career Development and Planning: A Comprehensive Approach*, 2nd ed. (Custom Publishing, 2005).

55 Mary Buzzetta and Shirley Rowe, "Today's Veterans: Using Cognitive Information Processing (CIP) Approach to Build Upon their Career Dreams," *Career Convergence Magazine*, November 1, 2012, retrieved from http://www.ncda.org/aws/NCDA/pt/sd/news_article/66290/_self/CC_layout_details/false.

56 Coert Visser and Gwenda Schlundt Bodien, "Solution-focused Coaching: Simply Effective," 2002, http://articlescoertvisser.blogspot.ca/2007/11/solution-focused-coaching-simply.html.

57 You can learn more about Melissa Martin and her approach at http://military2civilianemployment.com.

58 "Carl Rogers," Awaken, www.awaken.com/2013/01/carl-rogers.

Chapter 6

59 Roméo A. Dallaire and David M. Wells, Senate Subcommittee on Veterans Affairs, *The Transition to Civilian Life of Veterans*, June 2014, pp. iv and 11–12, www.parl.gc.ca/Content/SEN/Committee/412/veac/rms/01jun14/Home-e.htm.

60 See the Canadian Association for Prior Learning Assessment (CAPLA) directory at www.capla.ca.

Part IV

61 Pierre Daigle, DND/CAF Ombudsman, *On the Homefront: Assessing the Well-being of Canada's Military Families in the New Millennium*, Special Report to the Minister of National Defence, November 2013, www.ombudsman.forces.gc.ca/en/ombudsman-reports-stats-investigations-military-families/military-families-index.page.

Chapter 7

62 Pierre Daigle, DND/CAF Ombudsman, *On the Homefront: Assessing the Well-being of Canada's Military Families in the New Millennium*, Special Report to the Minister of National Defence, November 2013, www.ombudsman.forces.gc.ca/en/ombudsman-reports-stats-investigations-military-families/military-families-index.page.

63 Jason Dunn, Samantha Urban and Zhigang Wang, "Spousal Employment Income of Canadian Forces Personnel: A Comparison of Civilian Spouses," findings from Phase II of the Spousal/Partner Employment and Income (SPEI) Project, Director General Military Personnel Research and Analysis, DND, p. 20. Article available here: www.cfmws.com/en/AboutUs/MFS/FamilyResearch/Pages.

64 Jason Dunn, Samantha Urban and Zhigang Wang, *Spousal/Partner Employment and Income (SPEI) Project: Phase Three Findings and Final Report*, Director General Military Personnel Research and Analysis, DND, October 2011. Report available here: www.cfmws.com/en/AboutUs/MFS/FamilyResearch/Pages.

65 Dunn, Urban and Wang, *Spousal/Partner Employment and Income (SPEI) Project: Phase Three Findings and Final Report*, 2011.

66 Sanela Dursun and Kerry Sudom, *Impacts of Military Life on Families: Results from the PERSTEMPO Survey of Canadian Forces Spouses*, Director General Military Personnel Research and Analysis, DND, November 2009. Report available here: www.cfmws.com/en/AboutUs/MFS/FamilyResearch/Pages.

67 Dunn, Urban and Wang, *Spousal/Partner Employment and Income (SPEI) Project: Phase Three Findings and Final Report*, 2011.

68 Dunn, Urban and Wang, "Spousal Employment Income of Canadian Forces Personnel: A Comparison of Civilian Spouses," findings from Phase II of the SPEI Project.

69 "2-income Families Nearly Doubled from 1976 to 2014," CBC News, June 24, 2015, www.cbc.ca/news/business/2-income-families-nearly-doubled-from-1976-to-2014-1.3125996.

70 Pamela McBride and Lori Cleymans, "A Paradigm Shift: Strategies for Assisting Military Spouses in Obtaining a Successful Career Path," *Career Planning and Adult Development Journal* 30, no. 3 (Fall 2014): 92–102.

71 A committee of federal, provincial, and territorial officials, the Labour Mobility Coordinating Group (LMCG), exists to address the labour mobility challenges associated with these exceptions. The committee was established by the Forum of Labour Market Ministers. At this Forum, the Government of Canada is represented by the Labour Market Integration Division of Employment and Social Development Canada (ESDC). Military Family Services has met with ESDC to help support and inform this work, which can benefit all Canadians but particularly military families who are so mobile, and who move every two to three years on average.

72 Dunn, Urban and Wang, *Spousal/Partner Employment and Income (SPEI) Project: Phase Three Findings and Final Report*, 2011.

73 Jesse Carey and Lindsey Staton, "14 Maya Angelou Quotes about Living a Life of Purpose," Relevant Magazine, May 28, 2015, www.relevantmagazine.com/culture/14-maya-angelou-quotes-about-living-life-purpose.

Chapter 8

74 The Career Edge CAFR (Canadian Armed Forces Reservist) Project, sponsored by Employment and Social Development Canada (ESDC) has an optional subsidy available for Reservists (between the ages of 19 and 30), in the amount of $1,000 per month. The internship duration must be a minimum of six months ($6,000 subsidy) and can be up to 12 months ($12,000 subsidy). The subsidy is based on a 21-working-day month and will be pro-rated based on the total number of days in the internship. ESDC will provide the subsidy directly to Career Edge Organization (CEO); CEO will show this amount as a credit on the employer partner's invoice.

75 The Subsidized Education Plan is for CAF members and incurs obligatory service as part of their contract.

76 Funding for the growth of the BCIT program has been granted through Employment and Social Development Canada (ESDC) for the next two years. BCIT is looking to build a competency translator for military profiles using, in part, the existing CAF Accreditation Certification Equivalency database, www.caface-rfacace.forces.gc.ca.

77 Richard N. Bolles, "A Serious Call for More Career Development 'Mechanics' Who Can Help Returning Vets," *Career Planning and Adult Development Journal* 30, no. 3 (Fall 2014): 33.

Conclusion

78 Canada Company has convened an Education Consortium that is working on this issue.

Knowledge Champions

A special thank you to the Knowledge Champions for career development who helped to make possible the publication of this guide.

British Columbia Institute of Technology (BCIT)

BCIT offers an innovative new program dedicated to supporting Canadian soldiers who are transitioning to the civilian workforce. We have created an alternative approach to recognizing the skills and knowledge gained through military service by offering advanced placement into post-secondary programs, called the Advanced Placement and Prior Learning (APPL) method. www.bcit.ca/business/site

Canada Company

Is a charitable organization. Founded, funded and supported by the Canadian business community, to serve our military. A non-profit organization exclusively supporting the military with a direct line on the specific needs of Canadian businesses. With a proven track record of building unique programs that create opportunities for businesses to benefit from the strategy and discipline of military-trained resources. www.canadacompany.ca

Canadian Career Information Association (CCIA)

The Canadian Career Information Association (CCIA) was formed in 1975 as a volunteer organization of members from across Canada who work in the field of career information. CCIA brings together professionals who share a common interest in the development, distribution and use of career resources. www.ccia-acadop.ca

CERIC

CERIC—the Canadian Education and Research Institute for Counselling—is a charitable organization that advances education and research in career counselling and career development, in order to increase the economic and social well-being of Canadians. It funds projects, hosts the Cannexus conference, publishes *The Canadian Journal of Career Development*, and runs the ContactPoint / OrientAction online communities. www.ceric.ca

Fanshawe College

Fanshawe is a comprehensive college providing flexible learning arrangements in response to labour market needs. We offer more than 200 degree, diploma, certificate and apprenticeship programs helping people unlock their potential and achieve success in a variety of disciplines including applied arts, business, health care, human services, hospitality and technology. www.fanshawec.ca

G. Raymond Chang School of Continuing Education, Ryerson University

Enhance your career skills and get workplace ready with Ryerson University's G. Raymond Chang School of Continuing Education. Our practical, applied courses and programs are an ideal fit for your career transition or movement into a degree program. Choose from 1,500 courses and 82 certificate programs, in flexible formats suited to your learning style. ce-online.ryerson.ca/ce/

Marine Institute of Memorial University

It's a big world. Be at the center of it. Welcome to the Marine Institute of Memorial University. We're a world-leading centre for marine and ocean-related career education and research. A cutting-edge education from the Marine Institute is one of the most affordable in Canada and gives you credentials that are recognized around the globe. www.mi.mun.ca

Northern Alberta Institute of Technology (NAIT)

The Northern Alberta Institute of Technology (NAIT) is a leading Canadian polytechnic, delivering education in science, technology and the environment; business; health; and trades. With nearly 60,000 credit and continuing education students and a 95 percent employer satisfaction rate, NAIT grads are essential to Alberta's economic prosperity. www.nait.ca

TriOS College

For over 22 years triOS has helped students become job-ready graduates. triOS is a diploma-granting college focused on providing students with the practical hands-on training they need to succeed in their chosen field. triOS offers a wide variety of accredited programs that are highly relevant to today's job market within Business, Technology, Healthcare, Law, and Supply Chain. www.trios.com

WILFRID LAURIER UNIVERSITY

Wilfrid Laurier University

For over a century, Wilfrid Laurier University has been recognized for academic excellence through diverse, relevant and inspiring programs offered at each of our campus locations— Waterloo, Brantford, Kitchener and Toronto. Pivotal to the Laurier experience is our commitment to engaging all students in their career development as they prepare for the future. www.wlu.ca